FISH AND FISH DISHES OF LAOS

A facsimile reproduction of Recipe No. 103 from the Cahiers of Phia Sing. See page 120 for an account of these important documents. The recipe, which is for Pa sa ngoua tchun na som, is translated on page 153.

FISH AND FISH DISHES OF LAOS

ALAN DAVIDSON

with drawings by
Elian Prasith Souvannavong,
Thao Soun and Thao Singha

PROSPECT BOOKS
2003

This edition first published in Great Britain in 2003 by Prospect Books, Allaleigh House, Blackawton, Totnes, Devon TQ9 7DL.

Copyright ©1975, 2003 Alan Davidson.

Fish and Fish Dishes of Laos was first published by the author in Vientiane in 1975 and subsequently, also in 1975, by Charles E. Tuttle Co., Inc., in Rutland (Vermont) and Tokyo. This first British edition is a photographic reprint of the 1975 impression.

Alan Davidson asserts his right to be identified as the author in accordance with the Copyright, Designs & Patents Act 1988.

No part of this publication may be reproduced, stored in a retrieval system, or transmitted in any form or by any means, electronic, mechanical, photocopying, recording or otherwise, without the prior permission of the copyright holder.

British Library Cataloguing in Publication Data:
A catalogue entry for this book is available from the British Library.

ISBN 1-907325-95-5

The cover illustration is by a young Lao artist, a student at the Lycée Technique in Vientiane during the early 1970s.

Printed and bound in Great Britain by the Cromwell Press, Trowbridge, Wiltshire.

CONTENTS

Preface	7
Introduction	9
Acknowledgements	11

CATALOGUE OF FISH

Explanation of the Catalogue	15
1. Carp and Kindred Fish	19
2. Catfish	51
3. Perch-like Fish	73
4. Other Fish, etc.	85
Oddities and Mysteries	97

COOKERY

Notes on Cookery and Ingredients	103
Lao Recipes	121
Recipes from Neighbouring Countries	168
Appendix: the Pa Beuk	181
Bibliography	187
Index	190

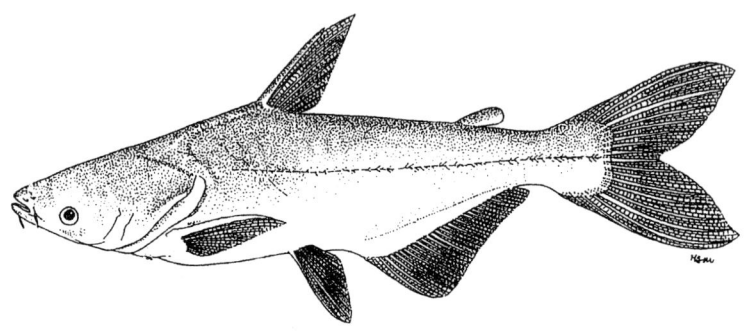

The preface to this new edition (see opposite) mentions an FAO book which includes a fine drawing of the giant catfish. This drawing is 'after Durand, 1947', and I have taken the opportunity of this new edition to include it here, since it is so much better than the drawing on page 66, which did not reproduce well.

PREFACE TO THE NEW EDITION

Just on thirty years have passed since the first publication of this book. It was an exciting event for me, all the more so because so little had previously been written about the fish of Laos. But then, in 1974, thanks in large measure to the research done by a Japanese expert, Dr Taki, and to wonderfully clear drawings of the fish by Laotian artists, I was able to produce something which would pass muster as a catalogue of those fish which are generally eaten in Laos.

There was no lack of interest on the part of Laotians; quite the contrary. The President of the Nutrition Advisory Committee, Princess Marina, kindly contributed a preface to the original edition, explaining the importance of fish in the national diet. This was considerable, but there were also other important aspects – myths, legends and customs relating to the fish and the fisheries. Everyone in Laos fishes, and the fish are perceived by everyone as not just a market commodity but rather as a priceless and sometimes mysterious part of the national cultural heritage. Sometimes mysterious? One need only read what I wrote back in 1974 about the giant catfish of the Mekong, *Pangasianadon gigas* (see pages 181 to 186) to understand the almost religious awe inspired by these huge creatures.

Mention of the giant catfish prompts me to draw attention to what has perhaps been the most dramatic development, of the last few decades, in the natural history of fishes of the Mekong Basin. I wrote, correctly, in 1974 that no specimen measuring less than 1.4 metres, in length had ever been caught, and that the truth about the habitat of the species and its way of spawning had still to be established. But then, in the 1980s, came the news that fish experts in Thailand had succeeded in breeding tiny catfish by the artificial insemination of a captured female. As a result they were able, at a later stage, to begin a programme of releasing tens of thousands of fingerlings into major tributaries of the Mekong. The prospect that the species will be able to survive has thus been greatly improved.

Since the giant catfish is the largest freshwater fish in the world, the preservation and enlargement of the stock is of particular importance, and not just for scientists and for all those people who exert efforts to maintain biodiversity, but also for the people of Laos, who believe that to eat even a tiny fragment of the fish annually ensures good health, and for whom it is a potent symbol.

The excellent FAO handbook *Fishes of the Cambodian Mekong* by Walter J. Rainboth, published by the FAO in Rome (1996) contains a fine drawing (see page 6) and provides a succinct description of the species, as follows:

> A Mekong endemic, growing to colossal size, now bred in captivity and widely introduced through Thailand. Shows one of the fastest growth rates of any fish in the world, reaching 150 to 200 kg in 6 years. Known to feed on algae and occasionally swallows algae-covered stones inadvertently. Probably also eats insect larvae and periphyton attached to the stones. A migratory species, but the actual distances and destinations of individuals moving through different parts of the river are unknown. Caught with seines and gill-nets. Marketed fresh.

So far, so good. However, as always with Laos and as indicated in the above quotation, some mysteries and uncertainties still prevail. I am grateful to Natacha du Pont de Bie for putting me in touch with experts in the region who may be able to give me more definite news in the future; and I hope that in the meantime any such news may be incorporated in Natacha's own forthcoming book on Lao food and culture.

INTRODUCTION

This is a small and simple book, but its several purposes require explanation.

In the first place it is meant to provide for English-speaking people in Laos an account of the freshwater fish which they will find in the markets (or indeed will fish for themselves if they care to join the Lao in this national pursuit). This account has a proper scientific base but is written so as to be comprehensible by all. It includes the necessary information on what to do with the fish before eating them.

A second purpose is to render a similar service, albeit in an incidental manner, for persons in Thailand, Cambodia (that is to say, the Khmer Republic) and Vietnam. These countries are all neighbours of Laos. Their freshwater fish are to a large extent identical with or closely related to those of Laos.

Thirdly, I have wished to make a contribution not to the art of cookery in Laos (which a foreigner would not presume to do) but to the small corpus of written material about this art. To this end I have included full and detailed recipes for the principal Lao fish dishes; an operation which has in turn required the provision of information about ingredients other than the fish themselves.

The people of Laos know their own fish and their own fish dishes. How then could they, by whose help this book was made possible, benefit from it? I hope that they may do so in two ways. It is often convenient to have in written form information which may be known to all adults but must yet be taught to children. Also, the coming generations in Laos, unless I am mistaken, will be increasingly concerned with the study, development and utilisation of their food resources; and for all these purposes will need more written information than they have now.

I should like to add a general thought about fish as food. We are all aware of the risk that the demand for food, in a world in which populations are increasing more rapidly than ever before, will outstrip the growth in food resources. And we all know that man does not live by bread or rice alone; we must have a range of foods providing for various essential needs. Our need for protein is perhaps the most urgent because it is potentially the most difficult to meet in a more densely populated world.

There are various sources of protein, many of them animal. Some forms of animal protein cost more, in expenditure of resources and in human effort, than others. Whatever our diet has been in the past, it is timely, at this stage in the twentieth century, to make such comparisons and to reflect on the changes in eating habits which may be forced on us if we do not by choice anticipate them.

The following statement by Mr D G Ginelly (of the University of Kentucky, in **Thailand, Inland Fisheries, An Overview**) lists the main advantages of raising fish, in comparison with other sources of animal protein. I read it during the energy crisis of 1973/74 and found that it provoked and iluminated my own thinking.

"1. Due to the buoyancy of the aquatic environment, fishes require less skeleton to support their bodies and therefore have a higher ratio of meat to bone, when compared to chickens, pigs or cattle.

2. Fishes (many species) feed closer to the base of the food chain, on algae or the lower animals, thereby conserving energy in the ecosystem.

3. Fishes are more efficient in converting their food to body tissue since they are cold blooded and no energy is required in maintaining body temperature."

Mr Ginelly provides also a list of disadvantages, of which two seem relevant here.

"1. Nearly all commercially important fish species are wild animals about which very little is known. This is a definite liability in developing fish culture when compared to the agricultural situation where plants and animals have been domesticated for centuries.

2. Man does not live in the aquatic environment, hence he requires specialized training and methodology for measuring various parameters before being able to interpret and/or understand exactly what takes place under water."

The advantages are fundamental and permanent. The disadvantages are incidental to the state of man's knowledge and may be temporary. The inference which leaps to the mind is that we should do well to accelerate the steady increase in our knowledge of fish and their environment and that all activities, however modest or unprofessional, which move us in that direction are well worth while; which is a pleasing thought for me, after writing this small study.

Vientiane   Alan Davidson
December, 1974

ACKNOWLEDGEMENTS

Let me begin with the lady fishmongers in the morning market at Vientiane. How patiently they have received my visits and questions; far more numerous than my purchases, but they never seemed to mind! Equally forbearing have been the officials to whom I have gone for help. From successive Directors of the Eaux et Forêts, Mr Khamdeng Sananikone and Mr Phouvong Vilaythong, and from members of their department in Vientiane (including, at an early stage, Mr Sisavang Chantepha) and in the provinces I have had, unfailingly, all possible assistance.

The work of Laotian officials and experts has in recent years been aided by the generous and well-devised programmes of USAID. It is under their auspices that Dr Taki has been able, in the course of his work here, to transform our knowledge of the fish of Laos. Where some seventy or eighty species were known before, the tally in his latest publication is over 200. In saluting this achievement, without which my own amateur work would scarcely have been possible, I should like to say what pleasure it has given me to be associated with Dr Taki himself and with his colleagues Mr Sugitani, Mr Suzuki and Mrs Chantala Khamvongsa.

It goes without saying that my thanks are due to all those who are mentioned in the book as sources of information or of recipes, and to the authors of the various works listed in the bibliography. However, I should like to declare here my particular gratitude to HRH The Crown Prince for having been so kind as to place in my hands the unpublished Cahiers of the late Phia Sing, and to Mrs Phia Sing for generously allowing me to use the fish recipes contained therein. I must also make special mention of Mr Thep Thavonsouk, whose dazzling linguistic abilities and culinary knowledge made my introduction to Lao cookery both rapid and extremely agreeable.

I thank here too a number of people for help not fully recorded elsewhere in the book: Miss Naly Abhay for material and advice on fish cookery in the South of Laos; Mrs Sisouphan Virasak and the staff and pupils of the Ecole Ménagère at Vientiane; Mrs Théothong Bounyavong, Director of the Domestic Science Section of the Fa Ngum School at Vientiane;

Mrs Thong Samouth; Mrs Phan Norindr, Miss Sommala Norindr and Mrs Vattsana Souvannavong; Mr and Mrs Thongrith Phoumirath for both translating recipes and advising me on them; Mr Thongdy Tassanaphol, for demonstrating the Pa beuk fishery to me at Ban Houei Sai; Jack and Marge Huxtable and the rest of the USAID team in that same town; Mr and Mrs Nguyen Huu Dang; Mr Ut Thai; Peter Ratcliffe, Martin Barber, Wyn James and Godfrey Dean; and the staffs of the Centre Culturel Français and of the Bibliothèque Nationale at Vientiane.

I am honoured by the compliment which the President of the Advisory Committee on Nutrition, Princess Marina Na Champassak, has paid me in consenting to write a Preface to the book.

My debt to HH Prince Souvanna Phouma for his encouragement and for his benevolent approval of the book is manifest. But I should add that many members of the Government which he heads have helped me with advice or information. Their Excellencies Mr Pheng Phongsavan, Mr Soth Petrasi and General Singkapo are among those who have enriched my knowledge by their reminiscences; and Dr Khamlieng Pholsena has exposed to me a rich vein of lore about fish in the South.

Outside Laos, I express my gratitude to the scores of officials, experts, colleagues and friends who have answered or furthered my enquiries, be they in Hanoi, Rangoon, Bangkok, Phnom Penh or Saigon. I must make special mention of Mr Chanintorn Sritonsuk, Director of the Nong Khai Fisheries Research Station, on the Thai bank of the Mekong just opposite Vientiane, for the neighbourly help which I have had from him and his colleagues.

I owe a special debt to Jacques Gaffier, not only for recommending to me the Lao artists whose drawings are the most attractive feature of the book, but also for his enthusiastic help and advice in planning its design. Here I avow some sympathy with McLuhan. Medium and message may not be synonymous, but the one can hardly be disentangled from the other. Writing, typing, editing, illustrating, designing and printing constitute a continuum of processes in which the author's hand is but one of many. With this thought in mind, I record my deep gratitude to Mr Chansamone Voravong, Director of the Imprimerie Nationale, and to Mr One Sy, Technical Director, and to their staff (notably Mr Khampheuang and the compositor, Mr Kongsone) for the interest and care with which they have produced the book and helped to mould it in so doing. Finally, and in the same context, I offer my affectionate thanks to Janet Lovelock for accomplishing, with great finesse, the conversion of my messy drafts into a typescript laid out for printing; and to my daughter Pamela for neatly constructing the index of fish names.

CATALOGUE

EXPLANATION OF CATALOGUE

The catalogue which follows provides illustrated descriptions of the main edible species of fish indigenous to Laos, with the addition of a few species introduced from elsewhere and commonly cultured in ponds. Over seventy species are catalogued and several dozen more are mentioned in the catalogue entries. The great majority of the fish which are brought to market are thus covered, with the freshwater shrimp and freshwater turtle thrown in for good measure. Even so, something like a hundred of the species of fish known to be present in Laos have been left out; and the reader is asked to remember that the catalogue is not intended to be comprehensive.

A LITTLE SCIENCE

Each catalogue entry gives the scientific name of the species shown. This takes the form of two (or sometimes three) latinised words indicating first the genus and then the species within the genus. Some species are shown with more than one scientific name. The explanation is that different naturalists have given them different names and that more than one is in current use.

The first scientific name given is the preferred name and is followed by the name of the naturalist who bestowed it on the species in question. Sometimes the naturalist appears in brackets, sometimes not. The brackets are used to show that the specific name bestowed by the naturalist has been retained, but that the generic name has been changed since the species is now assigned to a different genus. (This business with the brackets is the correct and long-established way of conveying information on this point, but one could wish that a method had been chosen less apt to give the layman an impression of erratic punctuation or haphazard type-setting.)

Where a generic name is followed by the useful abbreviation 'sp.', this means that reference is being made to a number of species in the genus together, or to a species of which the identification is uncertain. The only other abbreviation which requires explanation is C and V for the naturalists Cuvier and Valenciennes.

A species belongs to a genus, which belongs to a family, which belongs to an order, which belongs to a class. The introductory passages to the various parts of the catalogue will help the reader to keep track of the broader categories if he wishes; but any serious interest should be satisfied by consulting the more learned works cited in the bibliography.

THE LANGUAGES

The Lao and English names appear at the top of each entry. The former are romanised in what I hope is an acceptable way, but also given in Lao script. I regret that I am unable, at least in this edition, to give Hmong names and others in use in the northern parts of Laos.

English names present a problem. Most species do not really have an English name. On the other hand they mostly belong to families for which there is at least a general English name. Where such a general name can usefully be cited it is given.

Languages in South East Asia lap across the political frontiers. Even within Laos, and certainly in the neighbouring countries, it will be useful to know the names, where these exist, of the various species in Thai, Burmese, Khmer and Vietnamese. So these are presented in each entry. (The Khmer names are given under Cambodia. I know that the official name nowadays is Khmer Republic, but Cambodia is still current and fits the space better than the longer title.)

Laos has another neighbour, China. But I have not given Chinese names. There is a marked difference between the species found in China and those which inhabit the warmer region of South East Asia.

The heading Other is used for the occasional addition of names in the Malay language or from such countries as India, Indonesia and the Philippines, where these may be of interest.

Some names are given in brackets. This indicates either that they are general names or that they apply to closely related species rather than to the species listed. Some names are left blank. This means that they exist but that I could not find them in time.

NOTES

Under this heading I give information about the length of each species. This is normally what is called the Standard Length, i.e. it does not include the tail fin. I also give information about colour and markings and such other features as are likely to supplement the illustrations in helping the layman to identify the fish. I have avoided using technical terms so far as possible. The drawing on the next page is intended to explain those few which I have used.

Of course a scientist would give a different description of the fish, with less emphasis on uncertain and variable features such as colour and more on the surer methods of identification; but these often involve counting scales or peering at teeth and other manoeuvres which the ordinary person is loath to perform. Those who seek precision and full detail should turn to the works cited in the bibliography.

It is well to remember that in many species the male and female differ somewhat in appearance; that the shape of many fish changes after a big meal or when they are carrying eggs; that the colours of the live fish may fade quickly after death; and that colours may anyway vary according to habitat or other factors.

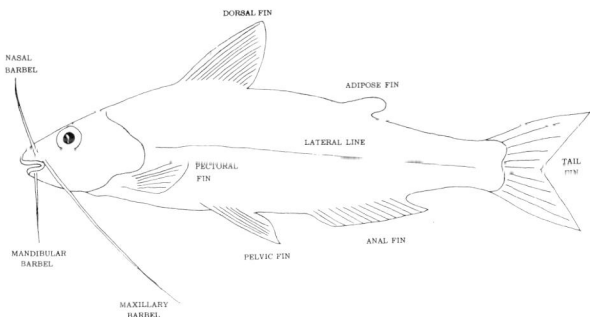

THE DRAWINGS

The majority of these have been done expressly for this book by young Lao artists from the Section Arts Appliqués of the Lycée Technique de Vientiane. The same artists did the decorative drawings which appear on various pages outside the catalogue, and the drawings which illustrate the cookery section. Their individual contributions are as follows:-

Elian Bleton Souvannavong did those on pages 6, 17, 30, 40, 41, 52, 70, 80, 88, 91, 92, 93, 103 (upper), 104, 106 (lower), 107, 109, 110 (upper), 112 (lower), 114, 115, 117 (upper), 131 and 163.

Thao Soun did those on pages 20, 21, 24, 35, 36, 37, 42, 45, 46, 53, 55, 60, 63, 67, 68, 72, 79, 83, 87 (upper), 95, 96, 101, 105, 106 (upper), 108, 110 (lower) and 112 (upper).

Thao Singha did those on pages 18, 22, 32, 39, 43, 44, 56, 66, 82, 86, 95, 103 (lower), 113 and 117 (lower).

The first two artists were also responsible for the cover of the book.

The remaining drawings are from published sources, notably Smith's **Freshwater Fishes of Siam** (drawings on pgaes 26, 28, 29, 31, 38, 47, 54, 64, 65, 69 and 81); **Illustrations of Some Freshwater Fishes of the Mekong Delta, Vietnam** (drawings on pages 23, 27, 33, 57, 58, 71, 76, 84, 93 and 94); **Common Food Fishes of Taiwan** (drawings on pages 48, 49, 50 and 85); and **Poissons des campagnes du 'de Lanessan'** (drawings on pages 74 and 78 - these are black and white reproductions of the finest colour illustrations ever to be published of fish in Indochina).

CUISINE

Finally, each catalogue entry has a section on Cuisine, in which I say something about the quality of the fish and the ways in which it is prepared. References are made where appropriate to the recipes which appear in the second part of the book.

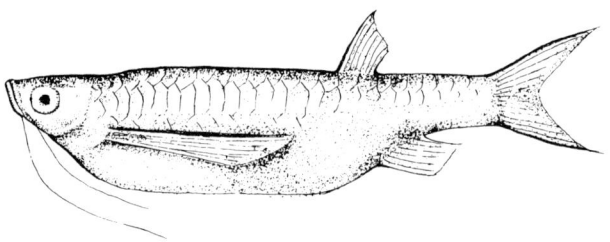

A fish of the genus **Esomus** (see page 22)

1. CARP AND KINDRED FISH

The family **Cyprinidae** is the family of carp, and it is a large one. About 1500 species are known, in North America, Europe, Africa and Asia.

Carp are fish of conventional appearance. Most of them could (and often do) figure in textbooks as typical fish. Their bodies are only moderately compressed, in other words reasonably plump. Their upper and lower profiles are usually both convex. The tail fin is forked and symmetrical. The dorsal fin is prominent and stands alone (there is no adipose fin). The head is without scales and the body is uniformly scaled, often with very large scales.

Even so there are wide variations between the species. In size, for example, the range is from tiny goldfish to the largest of the Indian Mahseers and the huge **Catlocarpio siamensis** Boulenger of S E Asia, which may reach lengths of 2 metres 50 and 3 metres respectively.

Carp have been important as food since antiquity; and have become all the more so because of the ease with which certain species can be transplanted from one region to another. Thus **Cyprinus carpio** Linnaeus is a species which originated in Japan, China and Central Asia. It has now been introduced into many other countries, including the whole of Europe, parts of North America and many countries in South East Asia. Not all carp are good to eat. Their quality may be affected by their habitat. It is commonly said in Europe that carp have a muddy taste; evidently because many carp there live and feed in muddy waters. Moreover, their diet varies. The Chinese grass-eating carp, another species which has been introduced into Laos and many other countries, is unusual in being strictly herbivorous.

Along with the family of carp proper I treat in this section the family **Cobitidae**, which contains the loaches, a group of carp-like fish characterised by long narrow bodies and low-slung mouths surrounded by numerous barbels. Like the catfish, the loaches lack scales.

PA TEP   ປາ ແຕບ   GLASS FISH

Oxygaster oxygasteroides oxygasteroides (Bleeker)
Chela oxygastroides

NOTES Maximum length 20 cm.

This small silvery fish (which has a brownish or greenish tint to it) may stand as the representative of a number of similar species, which it would be tedious to catalogue individually.

Thailand : Pla paep, Pla paep khao

Cambodia : Trey slek russey

Vietnam : Cá lành canh

Both the Lao and the Thai names mean thin fish. The Lao name is sometimes given as Pa thep.

CUISINE Although these fish are small, they are widely consumed in the villages. They may be seen for sale in the markets, ready-cooked; lots of the little creatures are held side by side in a piece of split bamboo, each fish with a sliver of bamboo protruding from its mouth. (These slivers go right through to the tail. Their purpose is to keep the fish straight while they are being roasted.)

Pa tep are good for Tieo pa ka tao (page 164), and are also used extensively for making padek. (I add here that Pa soi are even more popular for this last purpose. These are the smaller species of **Cirrhinus** sp., as explained on page 33; but the name appears to have a wider application. Indeed Seréne said that it could be used of all kinds of little fish.)

PA HANG FA   ປາ ຫ້າງຝ້າ

Macrochirichthys macrochirus   (C and V)

NOTES Maximum length just over 50 cm, usual length 30 to 40 cm.

A thin fish, silvery in colour and of a distinctive shape to which both Thai names refer (dab lao means Lao sword and pak pra means knife sheath).

Thailand :   Pla dab lao,
                 Pla pak pra

Cambodia :   Trey dang khténg

Vietnam :   Cá rựa

CUISINE The flesh is good, but fairly soft, and there are numerous small bones.

In Laos this fish is often grilled, or simmered with padek and made into Ponne pa.

| PA SIEU | ປາ ຊິວ | MINNOW |

Rasbora myersi Brittan

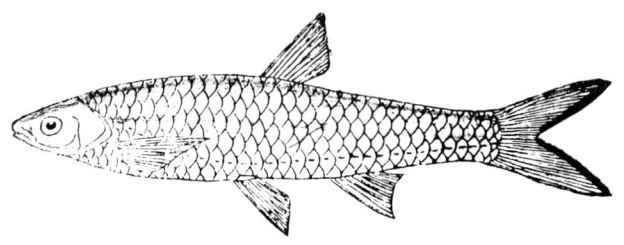

NOTES The maximum length of this species is only 8 cm. It is among the most common of the many species of the minnow tribe in Laos.

Thailand : Pla siew

Cambodia : Trey changvar

Vietnam : Cá lòng tong

These fish are in general appearance not unlike sardines. **Rasbora myersi** is a silver fish, usually with a brown back. The rear edge of the tail fin is black, as shown in the drawing. Another very common species is **Esomus metallicus** Ahl, a larger minnow which is pale brown in colour with a silver sheen. It is not shown, but the drawing at the foot of page 18 is of a fish of the genus **Esomus** and gives a good idea of what it looks like.

The Pa sieu in general have the reputation of twittering in the water, in circumstances described on page 25.

CUISINE These minnows are rather small for eating, but nonetheless have a place in the diet of South East Asian people. The larger ones may be scaled, gutted and fried. In Laos the smaller ones are cooked whole, with nam pa, herbs and citronella, in a package made of banana leaf. The whole package is roasted for 20 minutes or so on a charcoal fire. The contents (except for the citronella stalks) are then eaten with sticky rice.

The tiny creatures may also be eaten alive (page 154) or salted and prepared in the manner of Xhieng Khouang (page 150).

PA SIEU AO ປາ ຊີວອ້າວ MINNOW

Luciosoma bleekeri Steindachner

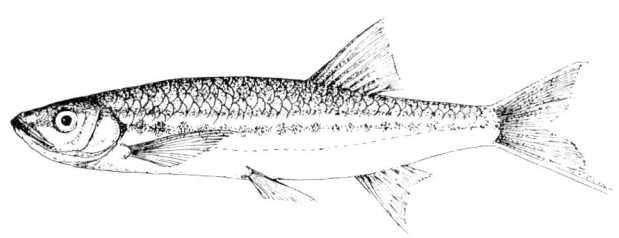

NOTES Maximum length 25 cm, or even more. This is a larger minnow, and a very common one.

Thailand : Pla ai ao

Cambodia : Trey dâng dau

Vietnam : Cá lòng tong miồng

The body is brownish grey with a greenish sheen, and whiteish below. A dark stripe or row of spots runs from the head to the fork of the tail fin. The dorsal fin is orange and the tail fin dusky orange.

This species has other Lao names, for example Pa sieu yuok and Pa sieu khao. Khao here means rice, in allusion to the fish being found in rice paddies. But there is a similar name, Pa sieu dok khao, which is applied to a smaller species. (Dok khao means rice flower, and this small species comes out of the paddy when the rice is in flower in September and October.)

The Thai name, often shortened to Pla ao, is interesting. Ai ao means a rogue or scamp; perhaps to Thai eyes there is something slick and potentially naughty about the streamlined form of this fish, although to me it seems beautiful.

CUISINE This is one of the larger minnows which may be scaled, gutted, and fried.

PA PHONG   ปา โพง

Leptobarbus hoevenii   (Bleeker)

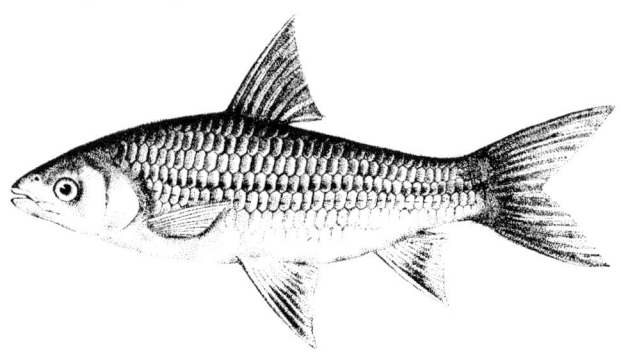

NOTES Maximum length 50 cm.

This is a river fish, and a handsome one. The basic colour is green, and the back gives the appearance of having been coated, over this green colour, with clear glass. A fish of this species, displayed in a window in the Piazza San Marco, would undoubtedly be taken for a supreme example of Venetian glass-making. A dark band runs from head to tail in young specimens but gradually fades as the fish attain their full size. The ventral and anal fins and the rear parts of the tail fin are red. There is an alternative Thai name, Pla hang deng, which means red-tail fish.

Thailand :   Pla ba, Pla ai ba

Cambodia :   Trey prâloung

Vietnam :   Cá chài

Smith explains that the Thai name means mad fish, "in allusion to its peculiar behaviour at times. When large fruit capsules of the chaulmoogra-tree (**Hydnocarpus**) fall into the streams, either directly from the trees or by being washed in from the banks by rains, the fish gorges itself on the parenchyma and seeds and is reported to become intoxicated and to behave in a peculiar manner. Its flesh then is said to be poisonous to human beings. As a food fish, however, its reputation is not high at any time."

The Lao name also means something like mad fish. The word phong is used of a person who is possessed by a phi (or spirit) and who will, for example, wander in the fields gobbling raw fish and snails without knowing what he or she is doing. These unfortunate people often go abroad at night, illumining the ground with showers of sparks from their noses, and may be recognised on the following day by the black soot-marks on their nostrils.

Altogether this is a most interesting fish. Serène observes that so far as Laos is concerned it is essentially a fish of the south, being rarely seen near Vientiane, rather more often in the vicinity of Thakhek, but well known around Khong, close to the Cambodian frontier. The Pa phong swim in shoals and are only fished in the Mekong, especially at the times when they go upstream (in January and February) and down again (in June and July). The fish going up are called Pa phong khunk; those going down Pa phong long. The Laotians, by way of explaining these movements, relate that the Pa phong make an annual pilgrimage to a big That on the Thai bank almost opposite the town of Thakhek, evidently because there is a relic of the Buddha there. To discover when they are arriving, divers go and listen underwater. When they hear the song of the Pa sieu, little fish which make a noise like crickets, they know that the Pa phong are not far away. "It is," they say laughingly, "as for the arrival of mandarins - one makes music." Serène adds that there is some doubt about the movements of the Pa phong, since some hold that they go upstream in the summer and downstream in January and February. (This seems now to be the accepted view, but a fish so beautiful in appearance and of so dark a reputation may well be capable of confusing fish experts as effectively as it alarms the minnows.)

CUISINE Smith's remarks, quoted above, are discouraging; and the Lao, except for southerners, generally avoid eating this fish and advise that anyone who insists on doing so should at least cut off and discard the head (in contrast to their normal insistence that the head contains the choicest morsels). However, the Lao in the south do eat it, and Cambodians prize it highly, for example for use in their soups Sngor and Khor. The Vietnamese even take the trouble to raise it in floating net-cages in the Mekong Delta area.

PA SOUT ປາ ສູດ

Hampala macrolepidota van Hasselt

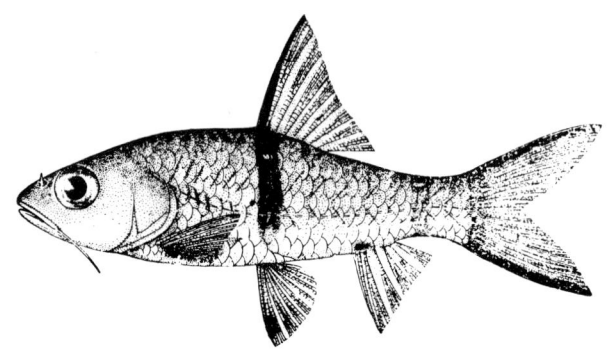

NOTES Maximum length about 70 cm; common length 20 to 30 cm. The largest of all are said to be in a pool below the Chendoroh Dam in Perah, Malaysia.

Thailand : Pla kasoop (or kasoob)*

Cambodia : Trey kham (or khmau)

Vietnam : Cá ngựa

Other : Sebarau (Malay)

The caudal and dorsal fins are red, edged with blue-black. The back is dark, the sides silver and marked by a dark stripe or blotch as shown in the drawing (but this fades in adult fish). Also, the large scales form a black trellis on the silver body - very chic.

This fish is abundant in the Mekong and in the Nam Ngum reservoir.

Hampala dispar Smith is regarded by some experts, including Taki, as a distinct species. It has a shorter tail fin, the upper lobe of which is smaller than the lower one; a black spot on the side instead of a vertical bar; and a much shorter pair of barbels than its relation.

CUISINE A good fish, although bony. It may be made into Lap pa. Informed that it could also be grilled, I tried this and am now in a position to advise against it.

*Commonly contracted to Pla soop or Pla soob; also Pla kasoop khao.

PA SA HO* ປາ ສະໂຮ **GIANT SIAMESE CARP**

Catlocarpio siamensis   Boulenger

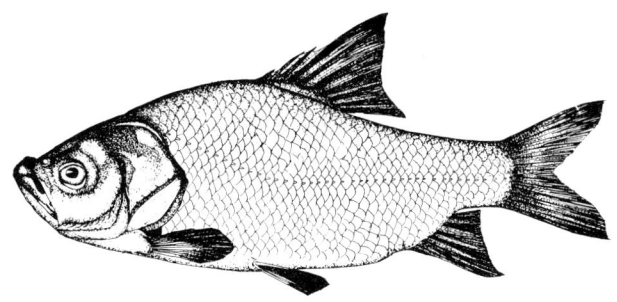

NOTES The largest Cyprinoid fish in the region and one of the largest in the world; there is evidence that the maximum length was as much as 3 metres in the past, and even nowadays it may be as much as 2 metres 50. However, market specimens are usually much smaller.

Thailand :   Pla kaho

Burma :   Nga thine

Cambodia :   Trey kolréang

Vietnam :   Cá hô̂

The head is broad and large. The body is burly and the scales are large and round. The back is greenish-black, the belly white and the fins red or orange.

The species belongs mainly to Thailand, but is also known in Cambodia and Vietnam as well as Laos. It is fairly common, after the Mekong has flooded, from Luang Prabang down to Pakse. Its capture and sale are, however, prohibited in Cambodia, for fear that it will become extinct. The Khmer name Trey kaho is applied to young specimens.

CUISINE Some people find this fish good when eaten fresh; others like it better pickled. In Laos it is considered to be of excellent quality for making Lap pa. Smith tells us that: "On the roof of the mouth just in front of the esophagus there is a large mass of adenoid tissue, and one of the earlier Siamese kings was very fond of this substance as a food morsel". I have been on the lookout for this morsel, but it eludes me.

*but the name Pa oun mo is used at Luang Prabang

PA HIEN   ปา ຮຽນ   CARP

Tor sp.

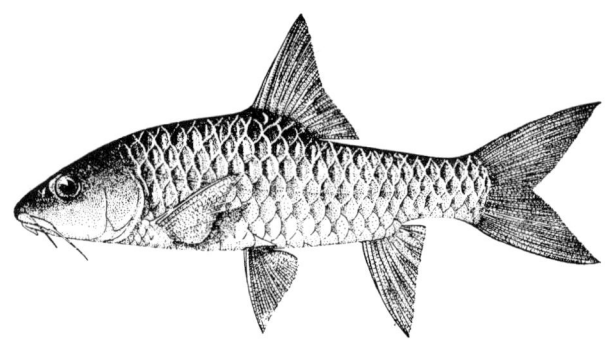

Thailand :	Pla kien (wien)
Cambodia :	Trey kaor
Vietnam :	Cá he

NOTES Several species of the genus **Tor** are found in Laos, as in Thailand, but the experts do not agree on which they are. This being so, I give only a general description, accompanied by a drawing of **Tor tambroides** (Bleeker), which is probably one of the species commonly found in Laos. The fish taken in Laos have a maximum length of not much more than 30 cm. They are brownish in colour, lighter below and darker above, and furnished with the pleasing silhouette and barbels shown in the drawing. **Tor tor** (Hamilton) is, by the way, the famous Mahseer of India (Nga-dok in Burma).

Serène relates that Lao fishermen often fasten pebbles to their line so as to mask the hook and bait. The Pa hien scents the bait and uses its snout to burrow under the pebbles, like a pig, only to be taken on the concealed hook.

CUISINE These are fish of good quality. **Tor tambroides** attracted the following comments from Smith: "The flavor of the flesh of this fish is delicious and superior to that of any other fish known to the people on Petchaburi River. . . . . . The largest fish are reputed to have the best flavor . . . .Fishing is done with a line armed with small hooks baited with a cake made from the fruit of the sugar palm mixed with rice flour . . . . The large scales are sometimes eaten after being cooked in boiling lard rendered puffy."

Pa hien are often steamed or used for Lap pa, but they may also be prepared in other standard ways.

PA TIOK (or TCHIUK)   ປາ ຈອກ   BARB

Cyclocheilichthys enoplos (Bleeker)

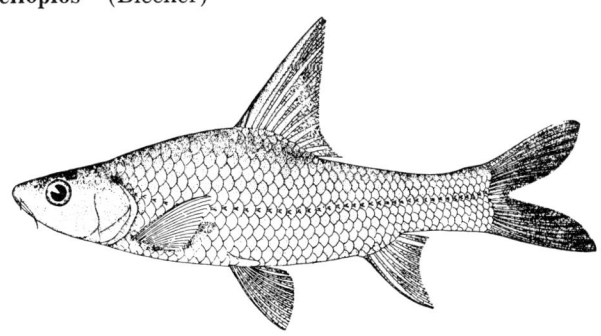

NOTES Maximum length 60 cm, common length 30 to 45 cm. This is the largest member of a genus which includes several other species.

Note the relatively small head. The body is silvery white, and the fins light green. The scales are large plaques. Beware of the long and strong dorsal spine.

Thailand : Pla takok

Cambodia : Trey chkok

Vietnam : Cá cốc

Cyclocheilichthys apogon (C and V) is a pretty little fish. Several rows of distinct dark dots run from head to tail along its light silver body. Small specimens (up to about 10 cm) are caught in very large numbers from the Nam Ngum reservoir at the beginning of the dry season. It is Pa tiok gniou in Laos; Pla nam lang, Pla sai tan or Pla tapien sai in Thailand; and Trey sraka kdam in Cambodia.

Cyclocheilichthys repasson (Bleeker) is known in Laos as Pa khao i thai. It is a brownish fish with a silvery sheen. Each scale on back and sides bears a dark brown spot, giving the effect of interrupted stripes.

CUISINE The flesh has a very good flavour and is therefore much in demand despite its being bony. (I met a lady in Phnom Penh who sees a necessary connection between the two attributes. "The bonier a fish is, the better it tastes," said she. It is not always so, but this species supports her view.) In Laos this species is rated excellent for the preparation of Lap pa and Som pa.

PA TIOK (or TCHIUK)   ປາ ຈອກ   BARB

Cosmochilus harmandi Sauvage

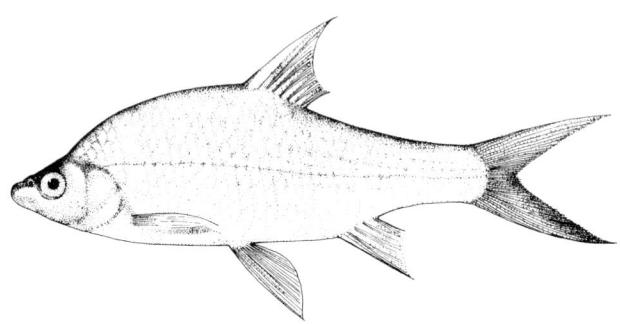

NOTES Maximum length nearly 60 cm.

This fish is of a bluish silver colour, with a darker back. The fins are mostly pale grey or grey, but the dorsal and tail fins are powdered with little black spots.

Thailand : Pla nam lang, Pla takok, Pla dog jok

Cambodia : Trey kampoul bay

Vietnam : Cá duồng bay

This is a river fish found also in North Laos. It is often taken with fish of the genus **Cyclocheilichthys**, which it resembles and with which it shares a number of vernacular names.

CUISINE A fish of good quality, used for Lap pa and Som pa.

| PA EUN | ປາ ເອີນ | CARP |

Probarbus jullieni Sauvage

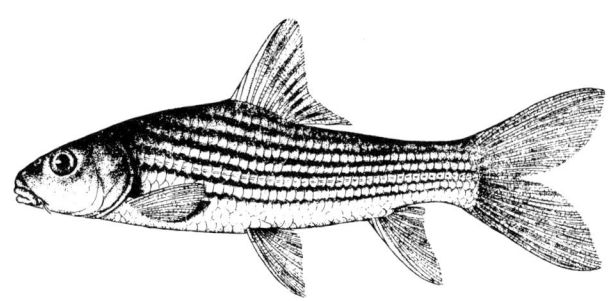

NOTES Maximum length 1 metre 20.

The body of young specimens is creamy yellow and marked by the black stripes shown in the drawing. The tail fin is blackish and the other fins pink. Older and bigger fish may acquire an orange tint; the body becomes less graceful, indeed portly in appearance.

Thailand : Pla yeesok

Cambodia : Troy trâsâk

Vietnam : Cá trà soc

Other : Temelian (Malay)

Trâsâk in the Cambodian name means cucumber, the explanation being that there is a sort of cucumber which is marked by horizontal lines in the same way as the fish.

This fish feeds on molluscs and is only found in certain localities. Indeed it is a relatively scarce species. However, experts in Thailand carried out successful experiments (in 1974) to induce spawning in the species; so it may be possible to increase supplies and to allay concern about its survival.

CUISINE An excellent fish with succulent flesh, of which the limited supplies are in great demand and fetch a high price. I suspect that the smaller specimens are to be preferred. (A steak cut from a very large one at Vientiane struck me as rather coarse and tasteless.)

A recipe for preparing the eggs of the Pa eun appears on page 159.

PA SA NAK   ປາ ສະນາກ

Barilius guttatus (Day)

NOTES Maximum length about 28 cm.

Thailand : Pla nang ao, Pla dogmag

Burma : Nga-lawa

Cambodia : Trey srâka kéo

A light brown, dark-spotted fish with a silvery sheen which is found in mountain streams in Burma, Laos, Cambodia and Thailand. The fins are generally orange, but the lower part of the tail fin has a dark upper edge. The spots are egg-shaped and arranged in one to three lines.

This fish is sometimes mistaken for a kind of trout. What is known as the Indian trout is a related species, **Barilius bola** (Hamilton), which also occurs in Burma but not in Laos.

The shape accounts for the Lao name. Sa nak is the name of the special hinged knife which is used for slicing betel nuts and the bark of the sisiat tree (which is what produces the red colour when betel nut is prepared and chewed). As the little drawing shows, there is a resemblance.

CUISINE Although bony, this fish is very highly regarded at Pakse, where it is taken in December and January, especially by night. It is used for making Lap pa and may also be grilled.

| PA PHONE | ປາ ພວນ | CARP |

Cirrhinus microlepis Sauvage
Cirrhinus auratus

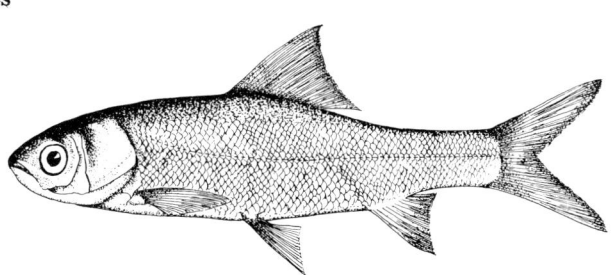

NOTES   Maximum length 65 cm.

A silvery fish with very fine scales (which, Hellei notes, are edible).

Thailand :   Pla nuan chan

Cambodia :   Trey pruol (or proul)

Vietnam :   Cá rói

It is a powerful swimmer and is able, like salmon, to make impressive leaps over obstacles. It migrates in shoals and is abundant in the Mekong, whence large quantities are taken during the months of November and December, i.e. the beginning of the dry season.

This fish is also well known in the Bangkok area, where there is a record of one which weighed 7 kilos, and in Cambodia, where it constitutes a high proportion of the annual catch in the Great Lake and the Tonle Sap.

The related but smaller species **Cirrhinus jullieni** Sauvage is an equally important food fish in Cambodia (where it is known as Trey riel). The Lao name is Pa soi, which is also used for a smaller still species, **Cirrhinus lineatus** Smith, which bears 6 to 8 narrow dark stripes running from head to tail along the scale rows.

CUISINE   Highly esteemed by the Thai and the Khmer, and in Laos, especially in the South. The flesh is fairly soft and of a good flavour, but it does have a lot of small bones. It is often used for Lap pa. See also the recipe for Pa chao on page 149.

PA PAK ປາ ປາກ BARB

Puntius javanicus (Bleeker)
Puntius gonionotus

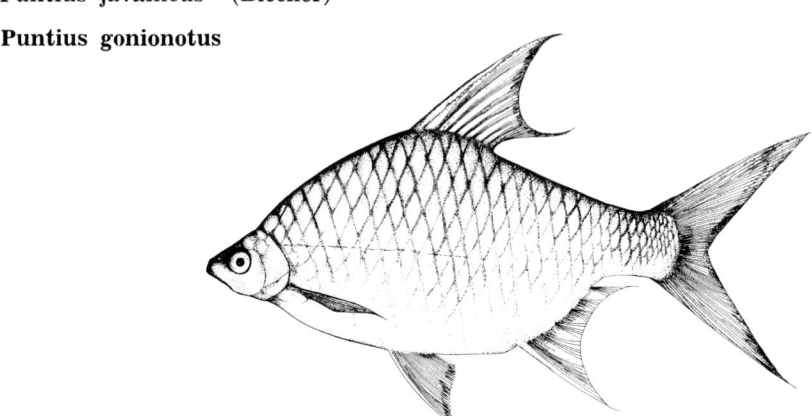

NOTES Maximum length 25 cm. A silvery fish with a darker back.

This barb has a fairly deep body, and its back forms an apex at the point where the dorsal fin begins. The same shape is exhibited by other species, such as **Puntius daruphani** Smith, a brown-gold fish with silver reflections and mostly yellow or orange fins, which is Pa pak kum in Laos and Pla tapak or Pla peek in Thailand.

Thailand : Pla tapien khao

Cambodia : Trey chpin

Vietnam : Cá trà vinh

Other : Lawak, Lalawak (Malay)

This is a herbivorous fish which can play a useful role in cropping excessive vegetation in dam reservoirs. Should the Pa Mong dam ever be constructed, this barb might do a good job in the new reservoir.

The Lao name Pa pak requires explanation. Pak means mouth; yet the barb appears to have a mouth of normal size. However, if a finger is inserted into it and pulled, the mouth expands outwards remarkably.

CUISINE The barbs are fish of moderately good quality, but they have a lot of small bones. They are therefore often used for Lap pa (in the preparation of which these small bones are ground fine and cease to be a nuisance). Or they may be grilled, or used to make Som pa.

PA LEUAN FAI   ປາ ເລືອນໄຟ   BARB

Puntius altus (Günther)

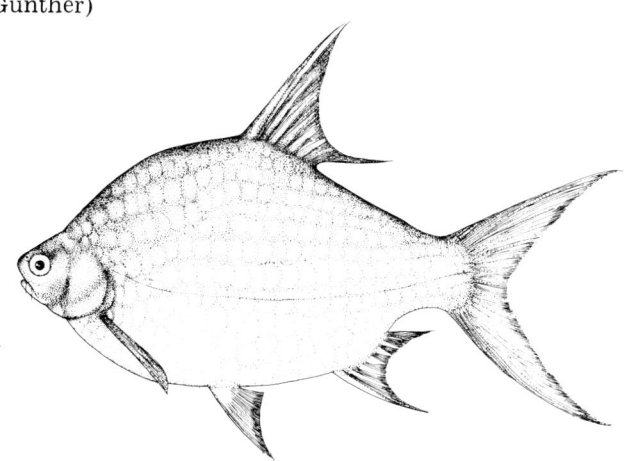

NOTES Maximum length 15 cm.

The body of this fish is silvery white; its dorsal fin black, the pectorals yellow and the other fins vermilion.

Thailand : Pla kapien tong

Cambodia : Trey kahè

Vietnam : Cá he

Fai in the Lao name means fire (an allusion to the red fins) and also occurs in the Lao name for a related species, **Puntius schwanenfeldii** (Bleeker). This is a silvery or golden yellow fish, darker above and almost white below, which attains a length of over 25 cm. The fins are red, except for yellow pectorals. The dorsal fin is especially brilliant and bears a black blotch. The Lao names are Pa vien fai (in the South) and Pa pak kham. Thai names are Pla kahae tong and Pla lampam. Kham in the second Lao name and tong in the first Thai name mean gold. Lampam is also the Malay name for the species.

CUISINE In general, see the preceding entry.

Puntius altus is one of the most popular cyprinid food fishes of South Vietnam, and is cultivated in floating net cages in the Mekong delta. It may be lightly fried, until it starts to turn golden, and then steamed and served with a nuoc mam sauce.

PA POK, PA KHAO ປາ ປົກ BARB

Puntius orphoides (C and V)
Puntius rubripinna

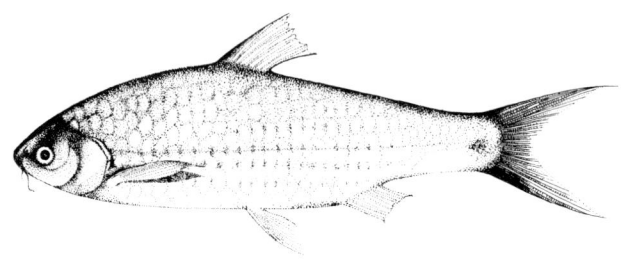

NOTES Maximum length 25 cm.

This barb has a body of more conventional shape than the others which are catalogued; it is not nearly so deep in relation to its length.

The Pa pok is a silvery fish with a brownish or bluish back. Most of the fins are red (with black marginal bands on the tail fin), but the pectorals are of a salmon colour. Various dark bands may or may not be present on the body.

Thailand : Pla kam cham, Pla pok

Cambodia : Trey ampil tum

Vietnam : Cá đỏ mang

Other : Marotja, Wadonon (Malay); Mata-merah (Indonesia)

Another Thai name for the species is Pla hao smoh muk.

CUISINE This fish is of quite good quality. It may be used for fish soup or for Lap pa.

PA SA KANG ปา สะขาง BARB

Puntioplites proctozysron (Bleeker)
Puntius waandersi

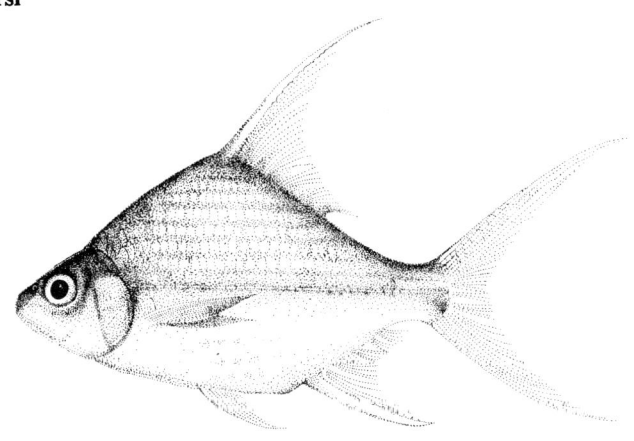

NOTES Maximum length 22 cm, usual length about 15 cm.

This is a plain silver fish, except for the dorsal fin and the trailing edge of the tail fin, which are darker.

Thailand : Pla kamang

Cambodia : Trey chakèng

Vietnam : Cá dảnh

The Pa sa kang is the only puntiid fish of Laos which has a large, bony and serrated anal spine; and this is why it has been placed in a separate genus. It may also be recognised by its shape, the apex of the back forming an angle of nearly 90 degrees and by its exceptionally prominent dorsal fin. An alternative name in Thailand is Pla liam, meaning angular fish.

The species is very abundant in the markets at the time of floods.

CUISINE As for the two preceding species. This one, which abounds in the Tonle Sap, is highly esteeemed by the Khmer.

PA KHAO MONG ປາ ຂາວມົງ BONY-LIPPED BARB

Osteochilus hasseltii (C and V)

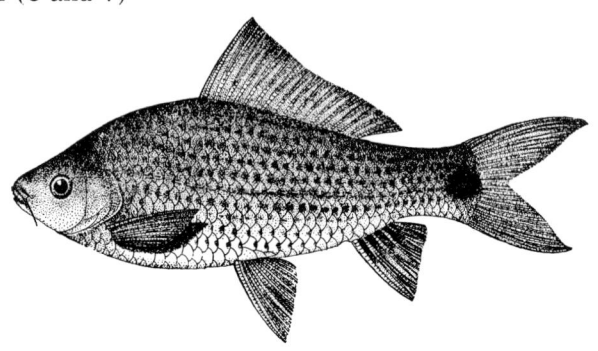

NOTES Maximum length 30 cm, usual length 20 cm.

All the osteochilid fish have bony, fringed lips and dorsal fins which extend for a relatively long distance along the back. This species is light in colour, silvery or greenish grey, with about 8 lines of spots (including little pink ones) running along the side and a dark blotch near the tail. Most of the fins are orange or red, but the pectorals are plain or greenish.

Thailand : Pla soi nok khao*

Cambodia : Trey kros

Vietnam : Cá mè

This is one of the most abundant fish in the Nam Ngum reservoir, where it is taken in large dip nets set on rafts. It is also a common species in Indonesia and Malaya as well as in Thailand and Indochina.

There are various smaller species in the genus, of which one of the most common in Laos is **Osteochilus lini** Fowler, a greenish-brown fish which has a maximum length of 15 cm. A larger species is **Osteochilus vittatus** (C and V), which attains a length of 26 cm and is dramatically marked by a broad black band running from head to tail.

CUISINE Quite good, but bony. It is used for Lap pa or grilled.

*The Thai names are interesting. Nok khao is a dove with black and white spots in the neck area. In peninsular Thailand we find Pla khi khom (bitter dregs fish) and in Patani province Pla tu bo, i.e. mackerel of the bo tree, which is associated with the Buddha.

PA NOK KHAO ປາ ນົກເຂົາ BONY-LIPPED BARB

Osteochilus melanopleura (Bleeker)

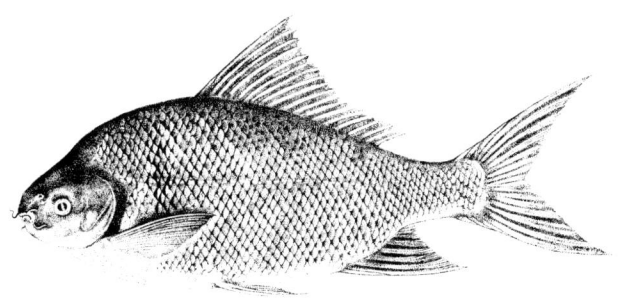

NOTES A maximum length of 50 cm is quoted for Thailand, although it seems to be no more than 40 cm in Laos. The usual length is 20 to 25 cm.

Thailand : Pla prom, Pla prom hua men*

Cambodia : Trey kroum

Vietnam : Cá mè

This is a greyish-green silver-spotted fish with black marks running up from the pectoral fin, like a fragment of trellis. Note also the shape of the mouth. It is curious that its Lao name should be the same as the Thai name for the preceding species.

Mention must be made of **Osteochilus prosemion** Fowler, the Pa keng of Laos, which is caught in ingenious traps by the people of Luang Prabang during the winter. It is one of the best known fish in the royal capital. It bears a dark cross bar on the 5th or 6th scale of the lateral line and reaches a length of 25 cm or so.

CUISINE As for the preceding species. It may also be used for Som pa.

The Lahu tribe prepare the Pa keng as follows. They slit it open ventrally, clean it and stuff it with a mixture in which the main ingredients are young fern shoots, lemon grass and dried chilli peppers, all chopped. They then close up each fish, put it in a piece of split bamboo and prop it up over a fire to be roasted. (The stuffing need not be eaten.)

*hua men - smelly head

PA KOUM   ປາ ກູ້ມ

Thynnichthys thynnoides   (Bleeker)

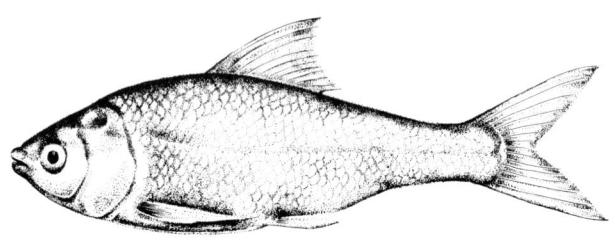

NOTES Maximum length 25 cm.

The scientific name indicates the tunny-like shape of this silvery fish. The Thai name refers to the very small size of its scales. Koum in the Lao name means short and round.

Thailand : Pla klet tee,
Pla nang klet

Cambodia : Trey kros memay

Vietnam : Cá linh bản

This is one of the most important fish, commercially, in Cambodia. An alternative name, Trey linh or lenh, is applied to it there, but may also be used of a different species, **Dangila siamensis** Sauvage.

CUISINE This is highly regarded as a food fish in Cambodia, although elsewhere it is thought to be only of moderate quality and somewhat indigestible. The Lao grill it or use it for Koy pa.

PA KHOUI LAM   ປາ ຄຸຍລາມ   CARP

Labiobarbus lineatus   (Sauvage)

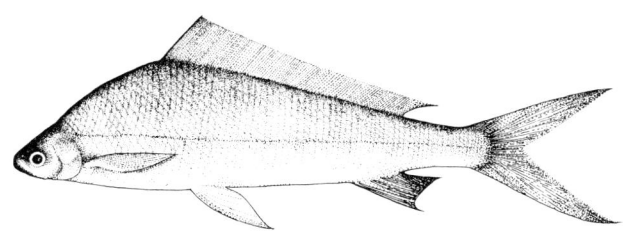

NOTES Maximum length **18** cm.   **Thailand :** Pla sa*

This is a bluish or greenish   **Vietnam :** Cá linh tía
brown fish with a white belly. The
scales on back and sides bear dark
spots, which give the effect of lateral stripes (hence **lineatus**). There is a
black blotch at the base of the tail fin. The fins are all brownish.

Note the very long dorsal fin. This is one characteristic of the
genus. Another is the fringed upper lip, which prompted the name
Labiobarbus. There are number of species in the genus but, as Taki has
pointed out, they have not been properly sorted out yet. This species is
called Pa lang khon in the south.

CUISINE This fish is a popular food in Laos, of moderate quality. It
may be used for Som pa.

Ripe eggs of this species are sold, lightly salted, in certain places
in Thailand.

*Pla sa is the general vernacular name for species in this genus. "According to some
information from Thai sources, sa may be an onomatopaeic name, representing the sound
made by the fish when they come to the surface and take in and blow out water and bubbles
as a part of their respiratory function. In the Tale Sap this fish shares with other members
of the genus the name Pla ta deng (ta deng, red eye). In the Badon district the vernacular
name is Pla lao tong (lao tong, golden spear)" (Smith)

PA PHIA ປາ ເພັຽ BLACK CARP, BLACK 'SHARK'

Morulius chrysophekadion (Bleeker)
Labeo chrysophekadion

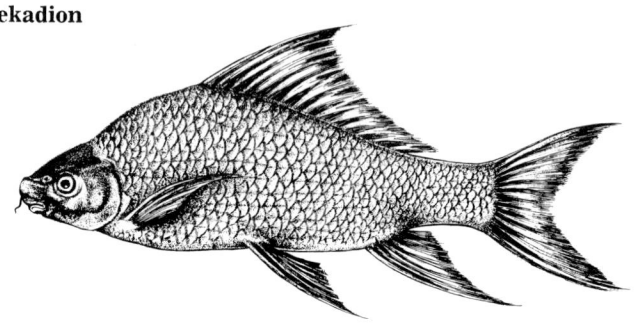

NOTES Maximum length up to 70 cm.

The Thai and Cambodian names mean 'crow fish', in allusion to its sombre colour. The scales, however, have a red tint which is apparent in certain conditions. The size of the dorsal fin is remarkable. All the fins are black.

Thailand : Pla ka

Cambodia : Trey ka-êk

Vietnam : Cá ét

Other : Si hatam (Indonesia)

This fish, well-known throughout S E Asia, is the most important member of the carp family in Laos, where it is mainly fished in the late summer when the rivers are running high.

The Lao name refers to the black liquid (with a greenish tint) found in the intestines of buffaloes and cows. Some Lao like to use this liquid when preparing lap from the flesh of these animals.

CUISINE A fish of good quality, which may be prepared in a wide variety of ways.

In Laos it may be used for Lap pa; or the head may be steamed and served with a sauce. It is less esteemed in Thailand.

PA VA   ປາ ຫວ້າ   CARP

Labeo dyocheilus (McClelland)

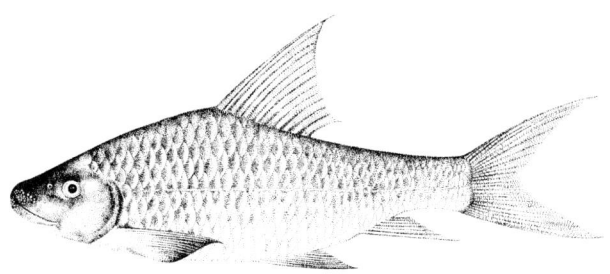

NOTES Maximum length 45 cm, although after talking to fishermen at Luang Prabang one would think that it is sometimes much bigger.

Thailand : Pla bua (lotus fish)

Other : Boalla (Hindi); Heel-gorya (Assam)

This species has a subtle colouration, which is difficult to define. The scales are brown with bluish or greyish edges; but the general effect is often best described as a misty and subdued lilac.

This fish is well-known in India, being common in the Himalayas up to Sikkim and in Assam. It grows to almost a metre in length there. In Burma there are related species of commercial importance, notably **Labeo rohita** (Hamilton), known as Nga-myit-chin.

The Pa va is the favourite quarry of HRH The Crown Prince when he goes fishing in the vicinity of Luang Prabang. He has described to me how a fortunate fisherman may sometimes catch three at once while they are performing their 'danse d'amour' (in which two males rub themselves, one on each side, against a female, in order to squeeze out the eggs). This happens when the Pa va come down the tributaries, in July and August, to spawn in the Mekong.

CUISINE Luang Prabang recipes for this fish are given on pages 123 and 158. I have also fried thick fillets, cut from the side, and found them good with a Vietnamese nuoc mam sauce.

PA SA I ປາ ສະຊີ CARP

Mekongina erythrospila Fowler

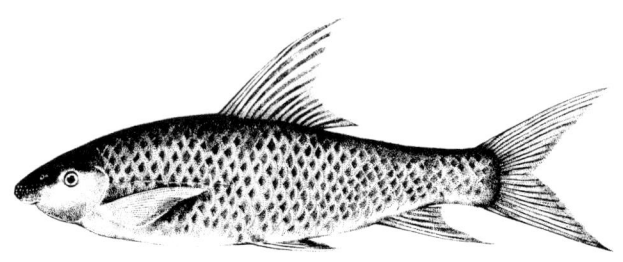

NOTES Maximum length 35 cm. **Thailand :** ?

The general colour of this fish is brown or greyish brown, each scale bearing a pinkish spot. I have noticed also rather more striking marks, also pinkish, on the 'shoulder'. The fins are dusky orange.

The species is closely related to **Labeo dyocheilus** (see the preceding page) and is sometimes called Pa va sa i. While on the subject of these names I should mention that Pa va ho kham is a smaller species of the genus **Labeo**, namely **Labeo behri** Fowler; and that Pa va souang (or souam?) is apparently a name sometimes used for **Labeo dyocheilus** itself. Serène also cites the name Pa va khai, and I have heard the name Pa va na no, but it is not clear to what fish either is applied.

CUISINE "One may do anything with this fish," says Mr Ut Thai, whose favourite it is. It may be grilled, or used in Som pa, Mok pa, Lap pa - the lot. However, it is considered to be especially good in Koy pa.

PA KO or PA KOR or PA HAK KUEY* ปา เฏาะ

Gyrinocheilus aymonieri (Tirant)

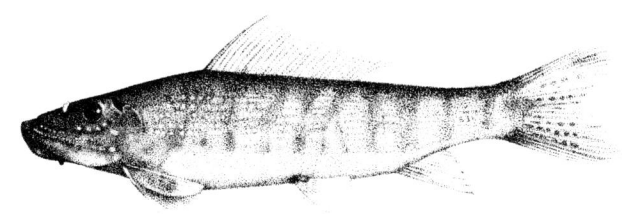

NOTES Maximum length 20 cm (or over 25 cm, in Thailand).

Thailand : Pla rak kluey

Cambodia : Trey bandaul chek

This is a brown fish with a bluish tint on the back. Three rows of about a dozen oval dark spots (which may run into each other) run along each side. But the pattern varies with age. The fins are yellow or yellowish brown, with numerous small dark spots, especially on the tail fin. The Lao word ko or kor refers to the small 'hook' on the head.

This species belong primarily (but not exclusively) to mountain areas. It is a vegetarian fish, scraping algae from stones with rasp-like lip surfaces (which also enable it to adhere to stones in swift-flowing mountain streams). Since its mouth is fully employed in rasping and sucking, this fish is equipped with an additional aperture above the gill-opening, so that it can take in water for breathing without interrupting its other activities.

CUISINE This fish may be grilled, made into soup, used for **Padek** or treated according to the recipe for Mok pa. See also the recipe for **Mam pa kor** on page 140.

*Hak means root and kuey means banana. The Thai name cited aboved also reflects the idea that this fish resembles a banana root. Other Thai names recorded by Smith are Pla piing (bee fish, because they swarm like bees), Pla pak lai (lower-mouth fish), and Pla muod.

PA KIEO KAI ปา แຂ້ວໄກ່ LOACH

Botia hymenophysa (Bleeker)

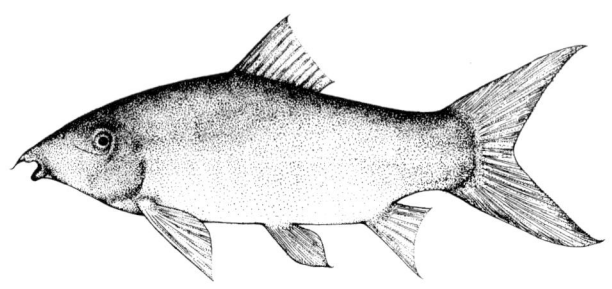

NOTES Maximum length 25 cm. common length 12 to 15 cm.

A beautiful and brightly coloured fish; but the colouration varies with age. A light brown or yellowish body with a darker back, from which descend 11 vertical blue or blue-black bands, is typical. The fins are orange or yellow.

Thailand : Pla mu*, Pla mu kang lai

Cambodia : Trey kanchrut

Vietnam : Cá heo

Botia modesta Bleeker, which attains a similar length, is also richly and variably coloured; but in this species it is only the young which display vertical bands. The fins of adult fish are orange/red. It is Pla mu khao in Thailand and Kanchrouk kraham in Cambodia. In Laos it is called Pa mou, mou meaning wild boar (an allusion to the 'tusks' of the fish) or Pa mou mang, mang meaning giraffe and being added in allusion (I supppose) to the stripes.

CUISINE These are fish of medium quality which may be used for fish soup or Som pa. The larger specimens may be grilled.

*Pla mu means hog-fish, in allusion to an erectile spine which is reminiscent of the tusk of a hog.

| PA IT | ປາ ສິດ | LOACH |

Acanthopsis choirorhynchos   (Bleeker)

NOTES Maximum length 23 cm.

This fish thrives best in swift, clear streams with sandy or gravel bottoms. Its colour varies, but is generally adapted to concealing its presence in this sort of habitat. A light brown body, with 16 small dark cross-bars on the back, and a brown streak with about 10 brown spots along the lateral line, is common. The fins are pale brown.

Thailand :   Pla sai, Pla kluey

Cambodia :   Trey ruschek

Vietnam :   Cá heo

Other :   Pasir

When this fish is frightened it will bury itself rapidly in sand. The first Thai name means 'sand fish' and the second 'banana fish'. The first name may be enlarged to Pla son sai (son meaning arrow).

CUISINE This is a fish of good quality, which may be used with excellent results in Som pa. Note, however, that the Lao absolutely forbid smoking when Som pa is being made from fish of this species, believing that even the tiniest shred of tobacco ash in the mixture will turn it bad, indeed make it harmful. Pa it may also be used for Mok pa or Or pa.

PA NAI ປາ ໄນ COMMON CARP

Cyprinus carpio Linnaeus

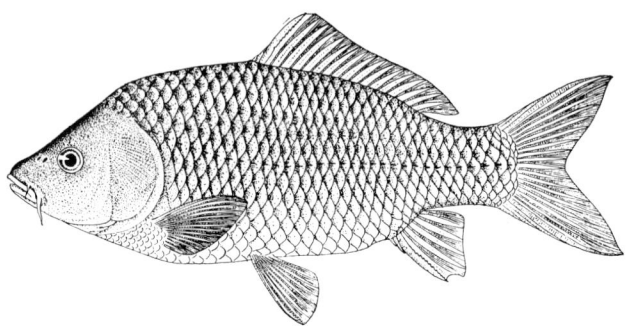

NOTES Maximum length over 60 cm. Usual market length around 25 cm.

The common carp occurs naturally in the north of Laos (and also in northern Vietnam, especially what used to be Tonkin, but the specimens on sale in most Lao markets are cultured ones.

Thailand : Pa nay

Cambodia : Trey srokchen

Vietnam : Cá chép

Other : Cá gáy is another Annamite name

The culture of this carp has a long history, starting in China. Thus Fan Lai, in his Book of Fish Culture (475 B. C.) wrote that there were five ways to acquire wealth, of which the culture of carp in ponds was one. More recently, the practice has spread to Europe (in the 16th century), Russia (in the 18th) and North America (in the 19th).

The common carp is a handsome fish, with a variable colouration. Specimens marketed in Laos are usually silver - grey, but sometimes of a yellowish or even golden hue.

CUISINE This is a fish of good quality, and firm flesh with which cooks both oriental and occidental have long been accustomed to perform culinary feats, in many of which a sweet - sour note is struck to good effect. (cf Jane Grigson's presentation of some European carp recipes in **Fish Cookery**, David and Charles, 1973). In Laos it is usually grilled or used in Koy pa, Mok pa or Nung pa (pages 130, 142, 146).

| PA KIN GNA* | ປາ ກິນຫຍ້າ | GRASS CARP |

Ctenopharyngodon idellus (C and V)

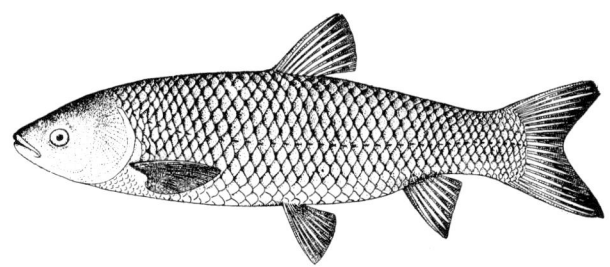

NOTES Maximum length said to be 1 metre 25; usual market length much less. A greyish-brown fish which is silvery-white below.

Cambodia : Trey srokchen

Vietnam : Cá chăm trẳng

The grass carp (properly grass-eating carp) is widely distributed all over China and has been introduced into many parts of South East Asia for rearing in ponds. It occurs naturally in North Vietnam. Chevey and Lemasson record catching it near Hanoi. But, so far as I can discover, it is not indigenous to even the northern part of Laos.

This and the two species shown on the next page are all sometimes known as Chinese carp. The three species may be reared together, since they have complementary feeding habits. The grass carp need only be fed on grass cuttings and grows rapidly. After one year in a fertile pond it may weigh as much as 2½ kilos.

CUISINE This larger carp may be used for Koy pa. Alternatively, proceed as follows. Cut thin slices of the flesh, lengthwise and avoiding the bones (which are to be saved for soup), and then chop these up into bite-sized pieces. Eat them raw, with a sauce made of nam pa (or nam padek, or Maggi), lime juice and scraps of hot chilli pepper. The Lao advocate taking alcohol with this. Looking at it the other way round, I suppose you could say that these little slivers of grass carp make good cocktail fare.

*The Chinese name may also be used. This is Chow hu. The Lao add their usual prefix and say Pa chow hu. But hu means fish just as pa does, so the addition is inappropriate.

PA HOA GNAY*   ປາ ຫົວໃຫຍ່   BIG-HEAD CARP

Aristichthys nobilis   (Richardson)

This is another fast-growing fish, which is cultured in many fish-farming operations in the region. The head is relatively large; the colour darker than that of the silver carp.

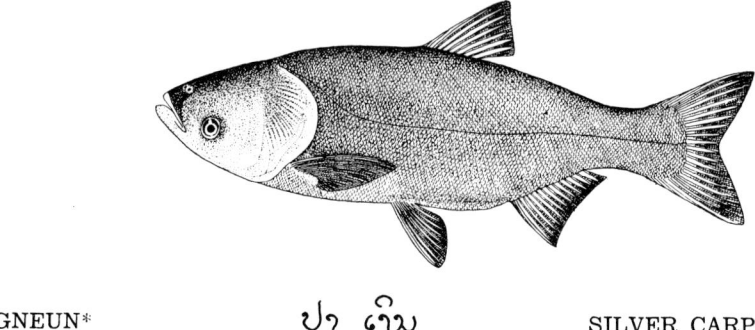

PA GNEUN*   ປາ ເງິນ   SILVER CARP

Hypophthalmichthys molitrix   (C and V)

This carp fetches a lower price on the market, but is still worth including in fish-farms. It feeds only on nanoplankton and does not therefore compete with other fish for the higher forms of plankton. Moreover, it actually improves the condition of the water in a fish-pond. It is greenish-brown above and silvery on sides and belly.

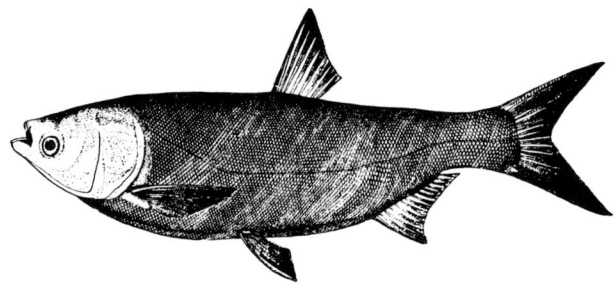

*See footnote on the previous page. The Big-head carp may be called Pa song hu; the Silver carp Pa lian hu.

2. CATFISH

Catfish are primarily freshwater fish, although there are also some marine catfish. The catfish are so called because of their 'whiskers' which are in fact barbels used for feeling around river bottoms etc in search of food. Another of their characteristics is that they have no scales. However, they are not the only fish to have barbels or to lack scales.

The name catfish is not honoured in Britain. Indeed, when the idea of introducing them into Britain was mooted, a rhymester in Punch wrote

> "Oh, do not bring the catfish here!
> The Catfish is a name I fear."

and went on to describe the fish as "a hideous beast, a bottom-feeder that doth feast upon unholy bait" and by other condemnatory epithets.

Americans have a different attitude, for they are familiar with catfish, including some of the best - the Channel cat and the Blue cat of the Mississipi. These prized creatures belong to the genus **Ictalurus**, which is indigenous to America. However, the best catfish of South East Asia are just as good. No Lao would ever admit that his revered Pa beuk, the Giant catfish of the Mekong, could be surpassed; nor can it be.

One advantage which all catfish offer to the cook is that they are free of tiresome small bones. But the quality of the flesh varies considerably and it is prudent to make an informed choice of species for your table, which the following catalogue entries should help you to do.

PA KHAO   ปา ค้าว   FRESHWATER 'SHARK'

Wallagonia attu (Bloch)
Wallago attu

NOTES Maximum length not far short of 2 metres; normal length 60 cm to 1 metre.

The back and sides are lead-grey shading down to silver, with a white lateral line showing up along the sides. The belly is white and the fins pale yellow. Note the very long anal fin and the long maxillary barbels.

Thailand : Pla khao

Burma : Nga-but

Cambodia : Trey sanday

Vietnam : Cá leo

Other : Jambal (Indonesia)
Tapah (Malay)

This is a powerful and predatory catfish with a wide distribution from India to Indonesia. Its voracious habits have earned it the name of freshwater shark, which is not however appropriate to it in any other way. It is abundant during the floods at the end of the rainy season.

Wallagonia miostoma (Vaillant) is a similar species which may be as much as 1 metre 75 long. In Laos it is called Pa khoun. Its Thai names are Pla tuk (or ituk), perhaps referring to its sombre colour (black or brown/black); Pla itub (itub means to beat, or splash); and Pla khao dam (dam meaning black).

CUISINE This fish has firm flesh, of a good flavour. It is the most widely consumed catfish of the Mekong, although popularly supposed to be unsuitable for women immediately after childbirth. The eggs are good too. It is the recommended fish for Gnu mak kheua (page 121).

PA KHOP   ປາ ຂົບ   CATFISH

Wallago dinema Bleeker
Belodontichthys dinema

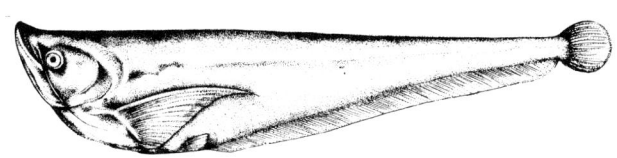

NOTES   Maximum length 70 cm; common length 30 to 40 cm.

The body is silver-white and iridescent, with the lateral line showing up like a seam of plain white stitching along it.

Thailand :   Pla biew, Pla kang buan

Cambodia :   Trey klang hay

Vietnam :   Cá trèn rằng

Other :   Lais, Begahak (Malay)

This is another common catfish, often found in the makets. It is as voracious as the preceding species. Khop in the Lao name means to bite or crack with the teeth.

The generic name **Wallago** was bestowed by Bleeker, who used the vernacular name from India for the purpose.

CUISINE   A fish of good quality, highly esteemed in Thailand. But the flesh deteriorates quickly after death, so it should not be kept for long.

In Cambodia it is used mainly for the preparation of Pha - âk. In Laos it may be used for Sousi pa or for Knap pa .

PA SEUAM   ປາ ເຂື່ອນ   BUTTER CATFISH

Ompok bimaculatus (Bloch)
Callichrous bimaculatus

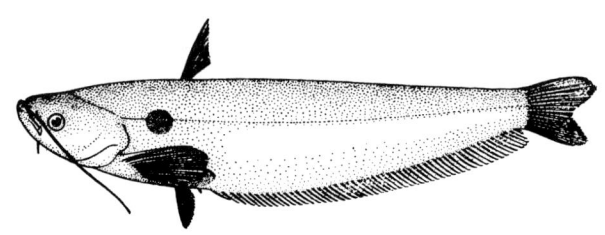

NOTES Maximum length 45 cm or more, market length about 25 cm.

The body colour shades from pale brown (perhaps with a bluish tint) above to white below. The body is sprinkled, as the drawing shows, with the tiny dark spots known to scientists as melanophores.

Thailand :	Pla neua on, Pla cha on
Burma :	Nga-nu-than
Cambodia :	Trey krâmâm
Vietnam :	Cá trèn bầu
Other :	Ikan laeh itam (Malay)

The range of this species extends from Ceylon and India to Indonesia.

CUISINE As the first of the Thai names indicates, this catfish has soft flesh. The Lao name of the species seems to have a similar significance, since souam is the name of prepared (white and soft) tapioca root. The flesh is certainly regarded as good, but it is to be eaten very fresh. It is suitable for Ping pa.

It may be smoked whole, in bundles with a bamboo stake through the heads; the natural slime of the fish keeps the tails stuck together.

PA SEUAM   ປາ ເສືອມ   SHEATFISH

Kryptopterus cryptopterus   (Bleeker)

NOTES Maximum length 20 cm.

The body is whiteish with an iridescent sheen. The pectoral fins are blackish, and the tail fin is often partly edged with black, as in the drawing.

Thailand : Pla hang kai,
          Pla neua on

Vietnam : Cá trèn mo

This species is very common in Laos and Thailand, and occurs also in Malaya and Indonesia.

Kryptopterus bicirrhis (C and V) is another common species, but slightly smaller (maximum length 15 cm). It has a white or pinkish white body, with a translucent patch just above the pectoral fin. This accounts for one Thai name, Pla krayok (windowpane fish). The Lao name is Pa pi kai.

CUISINE This is one of the most highly esteemed freshwater fish in Thailand, where it is eaten fresh, but also sold smoked. The flesh is tender, as the Thai and Lao names indicate (cf page 54).

PA SA NGOUA, PA SEUAM　　ປາ ສະ້ຽວ　　　SHEATFISH

Kryptopterus bleekeri　Günther

NOTES　Maximum length 60 cm.　　Thailand : Pla deng

The Thai name indicates a pink or reddish tint to its body, but pale brown seems to be just as common. The back is noticeably darker than the sides. Note that in addition to black edging on the tail fin there is also some at the rear end of the anal fin.

This species is found only in Thailand and parts of Indochina.

Another species, **Hemisilurus heterorhynchus** (Bleeker), deserves a mention here. It is generally similar in appearance to fish of the genus **Kryptopterus** and attains a length of 38 cm. It seems to be known only from Thailand (where it is Pla dong deng) and Laos (where it is Pa dan deng). Both names mean fish-nose-red, in reference to the reddish snout. The body is pinkish-white. Although this is an uncommon fish, it has an established reputation for the excellence of its flesh. "If you see one in the market," says Dr Taki, "buy it at once". (I did, and found the advice good.)

CUISINE　**Kryptopterus bleekeri** is a fish of very good quality, which may be prepared in all standard ways. See also the recipes on pages 148 and 153.

PA NANG   ປາ ນາງ   SHEATFISH

Kryptopterus apogon   (Bleeker)

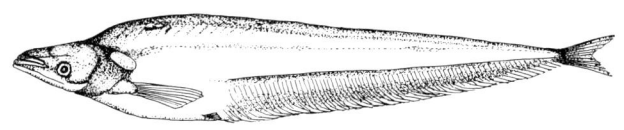

NOTES This species is said to attain a length of over 75 cm in Indonesia.

The back is grey, but the general colour is pinkish white. It is not easy to distinguish this species from the preceding one.

Thailand : Pla deng

Cambodia : Trey kès

Vietnam : Cá kết

CUISINE This is an excellent fish, even better than the preceding species. It is recommended for Mok pa and for Nung pa. Thai friends have served it to me cut into large rectangles and deep-fried, with a sweet and sour ginger sauce, and I found it very good thus.

It is often smoked in Cambodia.

PA DOUK   ປາ ດຸກ   CATFISH

Clarias batrachus (Linnaeus)

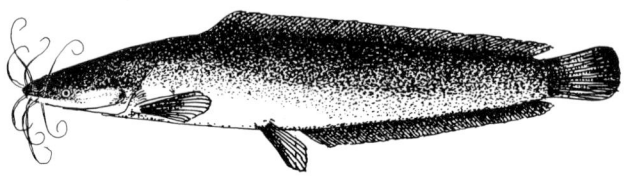

NOTES Maximum length just over 40 cm. The body is dark brown to black above and a lighter brown below.

This species has a wide distribution, from India to the Philippines. It lives in ponds and marshes as well as in rivers and canals, and can survive for lengthy periods out of water, so long as its

Thailand :   Pla duk dan

Burma :   Nga-khoo

Cambodia :   Trey andeng

Vietnam :   Cá trèn trắng

Other :   Ikan lele (Malay)

respiratory apparatus remains moist. Indeed this fish will leave water voluntarily, in search of better conditions elsewhere or to escape from enemies. The Thai name means dull-coloured wriggling fish, and wriggle is what it does to cover the ground, as explained by Smith in an entertaining passage: "The flat head and extended pectoral fins keep the fish in an upright position as it moves forward by rapid lateral bendings of the tail. On August 13, 1926, a friend brought the writer a fish that in the late afternoon of the previous day was picked up on a metaled driveway in his yard in Bangkok. The fish had left a small canal 15 metres away and was proceeding toward another canal 35 metres away. It was placed in a flat jar of water in the writer's office. It left the jar during the night (apparently by jumping), dropped from a table to the floor . . . , traversed a large exhibit room, went the entire length of a long hallway, and was found in a lively condition just inside the front door at 11 p.m."

CUISINE This is an important food fish. In Laos, for example, it is always on sale in the markets, kept in basins with a little water. The flesh is white and has a good flavour, but is rather tough and needs prolonged cooking. The Lao like to use it for Lap pa or for Ponne pa.

PA DOUK   ປາ ດຸກ   CATFISH

Clarias macrocephalus   Günther

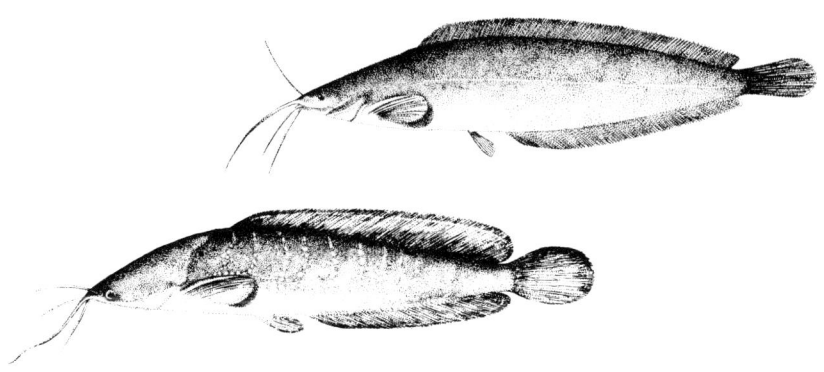

NOTE Maximum length just over 30 cm.

Thailand : Pla duk uey

Vietnam : Cá trê vàng

This species may be distinguished from the preceding one by its large, broad head which slopes down in an almost straight line from the front of the dorsal fin. It is less common in Laos than the preceding species, and the specimens which I have seen in Laotian markets may in fact belong to two species. Some are marked by vertical rows of pale spots, as shown in the lower drawing, while the others are not. The Lao certainly have three names for these catfish. Pa douk en is **Clarias batrachus**. Pa douk uey is **Clarias macrocephalus** without the spots. The fish with the spots are called Pa douk tassing (tassing referring to the metal studs which appear on Chinese balances, the kind that fold up into a little wooden case). Taki shows the spotted fish as **Clarias macrocephalus**, and it may be that this is a species in which individuals may or may not be so marked.

In Thailand many people think (wrongly) that it is the female version of **Clarias batrachus**.

CUISINE Both in Thailand and in Laos this species is considered to be better and more nourishing than **Clarias batrachus**. The word uey in the Thai name means fat.

SMALLER CATFISH OF THE FAMILY **PANGASIDAE**

This is the family of the really big catfish, to which we shall come in the next few pages. But it contains various smaller species, the classification of which is still giving difficulty. I present three of the more common ones on these two pages. They are all silvery grey fish.

PA NOU ປາ ໜູ CATFISH

Helicophagus waandersi (Bleeker)

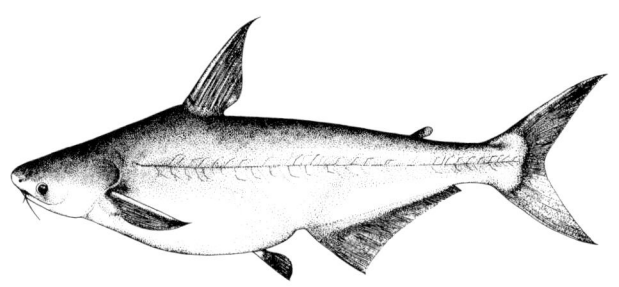

NOTES Maximum length 30 cm.

    This species is densely distributed in the Mekong and its affluents.

Thailand : Pla sawai nu

Cambodia : Trey pra-kandor

Vietnam : Cá tra chuột

CUISINE The Pa nou is a relatively expensive fish. It has quite a high fat content and is often used with coconut to make a rich Nam kapoen (sauce for the Lao national dish). It is also recommended for Pa chao (page 149) and for pickling (Som pa). When Lap pa is made with this fish it is known as Lap hot, and is very good.

PA LING (?) ປາ ລິງ CATFISH

Pteropangasius cultratus (Smith)

NOTES Maximum length about 30 cm.

I have not provided a drawing of this species, since it looks very much the same as the Pa gnon which is illustrated below; except that its barbels are shorter.

Thailand : Pla sangawart

Cambodia : Trey chviet siach

Vietnam : Cá sát bo

Thailand : Pla sangawart leung

PA GNON ປາ ຍອນ CATFISH

Pangasius siamensis Steindachner

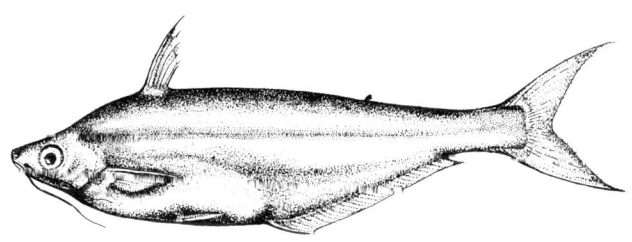

NOTES Maximum length 30 cm (but ? more in Thailand).

Thailand :

Note the advanced position of the dorsal fin and the dark stripe from gill opening to tail.

CUISINE Phia Sing gives a recipe for Knap pa gnon (page 129) and also recommends using this fish for Sousi pa (see the second recipe on page 162) and for Tom tchéo.

PA PHO (or PA PHOM or PA LING)   ปา เพ้อะ

Pangasius nasutus   (Bleeker)

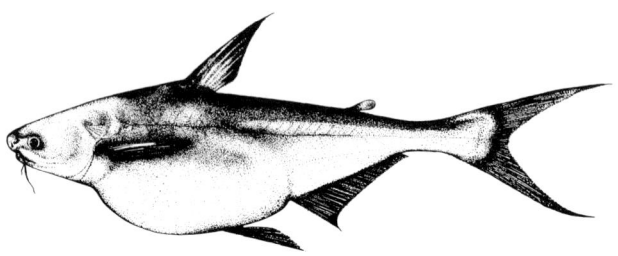

NOTES A maximum length of 90 cm is quoted by Taki, but in Laos the largest specimens seem to be nearer 60 or 65 cm and the usual market length less again (e.g. about 25 cm). The specimen shown in the drawing had a full belly.

Thailand : Pla saiyu

Cambodia : Trey ke

Vietnam : Cá tra, Cá ba xa

The same underslung effect may be observed in other pangasid catfish. It is a silver fish, darker above and lighter below. The fins are mostly yellow or white, but the dorsal fin is dark. The eyes are relatively small.

This species, which has a distribution extending to Indonesia, is abundant in Laos. It prefers a diet of molluscs, especially bivalves.

CUISINE Good, but not outstanding. It may be used for Koy pa. Phia Sing gives a recipe (not reproduced in this book) for Mok pa ling.

The Phousi Hotel, whose circular palm-thatched bar is the most agreeable place at which to eat as well as to drink in Luang Prabang (architect Christian W Lezy, to whom all honour) regularly offers Bar du Mekong on the menu. On successive visits I worried away at the identity of this fish, only to discover eventually what I might have guessed in the first place, that the flattering title is bestowed on several species, depending on which is plentiful in the market. I did establish that on one occasion at least the bar du Mekong was **Pangasius nasutus**; and the fried steaks were no less delicious because of the misnomer (bar being bass and bass being a far cry from catfish).

| PA SOUEI | ປາ ສວຍ | CATFISH |

Pangasius pangasius (Hamilton)

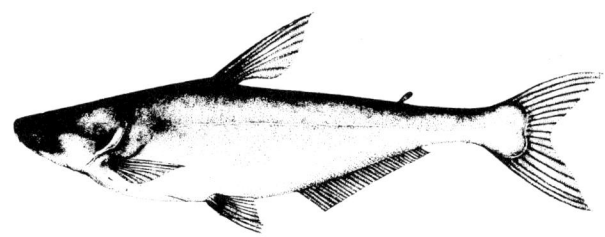

NOTES Maximum length about 1 metre.	**Thailand :**	Pla sawai
	Cambodia :	Trey pra
The back is light grey, the sides silver and the belly white. Most of the fins are grey or colourless, some with black tips; but the adipose fin is grey-green with a white rear edge. The tail fin has dark lines radiating out along the rays.	**Vietnam :**	Cá xanh kỳ
	Other :	Djuara or Djambal (Indonesia); Lawang is a general Malay name for pangasid catfish

This species is known also in India and Burma, and is reared for consumption in Thailand, Cambodia and Vietnam. In India it may reach a length of 3 metres. I understand that the largest specimens taken there have lost their teeth and are judged to be about ten years old. This sort of information is of interest in connection with the mystery surrounding the Pa beuk (see page 66 and pages 181 to 184).

CUISINE "The flesh of this fish is very white, fine-grained and sweet, and commands a ready sale." I agree with this quotation from Smith. This is an excellent fish by the standards of any country. Steaks cut from it may be grilled (preferably after dipping them in e.g. a mixture of salad oil and lime juice, so that they do not become too dry) or baked or fried. The eggs are good too. Ask for some if you are buying a piece of a female in the early summer. They look like little clusters of cantaloupe melon seeds and may be cooked by simmering them briefly in a fish bouillon.

PA HOU MAT      CATFISH

Pangasius larnaudii   Bocourt

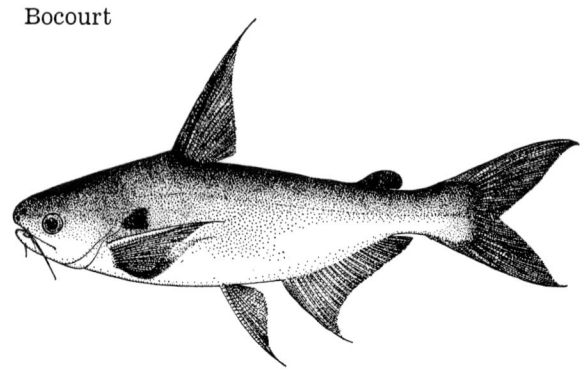

NOTES Maximum length over 1 metre 30.

Thailand : Pla tepo

Cambodia : Trey pau (or po)

The large black shoulder spot is a good recognition point. The body is grey-blue above and silvery or whiteish below; the head

Vietnam : Cá vồ

may have a greenish tinge. The dorsal fin is dark grey, the tail fin grey with a white rear edge and the pectorals pink. This handsome fish is peculiar to Thailand and parts of Indochina. It adores bananas and will take this fruit from a man's hand.

The naturalist Bocourt named the species after Father Larnaudie, who had helped him in his work in the 1860's. To emphasise the compliment he remarked on the excellence of the fish: "Its flesh is extremely nutritious and delicate; it is reared and fattened at Ayuthia in water courses which are enclosed by bamboo grills. Owing to its high price, the species does not appear in the markets of Bangkok; also it is reserved for the table of important persons."

CUISINE Very good. Yet in Cambodia this fish, although among the first twelve species in terms of weight caught, is used mainly for Pha-ak. Its reputation may be clouded by doubts about its feeding habits. Katay records that in the National Assembly of Siam a deputy abused his opponents with the epithet 'Pla-the-pho' ("peut-être parce que ce poisson de bel aspect . . . . se nourrit de toutes sortes de saletés"). The remedy is evidently to keep them in ponds and feed them on bananas.

PA LEUM   ປາ ເລິມ   CATFISH

Pangasius sanitwongsei H M Smith

NOTES Specimens 3 metres long have been recorded, but in practice the maximum length is more like 1½ metres, and the usual market length is less.

Thailand : Pla thepa

Cambodia : Trey po pruy

Vietnam : Cá vồ cò

The body is dark above, the belly white and the fins black or nearly so.

The species is found mainly in Thailand and Laos. The fishery for the Pa leum, like that for the Pa beuk, used to be accompanied by rites and ceremonies of a religious nature, well described by Archaimbault.

CUISINE This fish is less esteemed than its relations. The flesh is less good, rather fat and (for myself anyway) indigestible. People are also put off by the known feeding habits of the fish, which likes to eat the carcasses of dogs floating in the river. Fish merchants are said sometimes to cut off the characteristic fins of the fish before selling it, so that it will be taken for another variety with a better reputation.

The best way to serve Pa leum is with a strong sauce which will balance the fatty quality of the flesh. However, it should be added that the Pa leum is more highly esteemed at Luang Prabang, as the Royal chef's recipe for Khoua gnu pa leum (page 126) would suggest.

PA BEUK   ปา บึก   GIANT CATFISH

Pangasianodon gigas   Chevey

NOTES   Huge fish is what the Lao and Thai names mean, and huge fish is what this is. The maximum length is 3 metres; the maximum weight something like 250 to 300 kilos.

Thailand :   Pla buk

Cambodia :   Trey reach (royal fish)

This may not be the largest freshwater fish of the world (a distinction accorded in the past to **Silurus glanis**, a European catfish), but is possibly the heaviest, if not the longest, which can be caught nowadays.

This remarkable fish is only found in the Mekong and connected waters and has become rather rare. (The risk that it will become extinct has been recognised by its inclusion in the Red List of endangered species and by the banning of its capture in Cambodia since 1971.) It may be distinguished from the other large catfish of the Mekong by its lack of teeth and the almost complete absence of barbels. The colour is light brownish-grey above, shading to white below. There is a little white mark on the head, shown in the drawing on the next page.

However, the habits of the Pa beuk differ from those of its relation. It seems to feed only on vegetation in the river (although willing to take other food in captivity, as experts at Ubon Ratchathani in Thailand have shown). As for its general pattern of life and migratory journeys for spawning, these are so little known and present such fascinatin problems that I have dealt with them in an Appendix (page 181), which also contains information about myths and rites associated with the Pa beuk and about the fishery for it.

CUISINE Given what has been said above, it may seem inappropriate to encourage people to eat the Pa beuk. Yet it must be said that this fish is of superlative quality; and many Laotians believe that it is advisable to have at least one portion annually to ensure a long life and active old age. The flesh is of admirable texture and unmatched flavour. Like the flesh of the sturgeon, it bears some resemblance to veal; there are those who, tasting it for the first time, insist that it must be meat rather than fish. Yet it is fishy, in a subtle and majestic way.

Thin escalopes of the Pa beuk may be deep-fried or pan-fried successfully. But I think that the best treatment is to grill steaks over charcoal, dipping them beforehand in a mixture of olive oil and lime juice (which I flavour with mint, or thyme) and basting them during the cooking with this same mixture, to avoid any danger of their becoming too dry. The best meat, by the way, comes from the middle of the side of the fish, nearer the head than the tail, and is called sin sam (meaning bruised meat).

The liver is a great delicacy, sliced and grilled with a little salt. The head provides an excellent soup. But if you buy a head, as I once did, remember that it may weigh 50 kilos and that you will need to invite 150 guests. Pa beuk meat can also be used to make the finest quality padek (Padek pa beuk) and pickled fish (Som pa beuk).

The eggs taken from females are salted and provide what is called 'Laotian caviar'. This is reddish in colour and is eaten on rice cakes. It is prepared only at Luang Prabang. The recipe is like that for Som khay pa eun (page 159), but there are important differences. Ordinary rice, not sticky rice, is used, and it must be made ready by being steamed once a day for three days. Moreover, sticklac is dissolved in boiling water to produce a liquid which gives to Som khay pa beuk its distinctive plum colour. When I ate it at the Palace, it was served on a bed of spring onion tops and decorated with tiny red chilli peppers stuck upright in it like little tongues of flame.

PA KA GNENG*　　　ປາ ກະແຍງ　　　CATFISH

Bagroides macracanthus Bleeker**

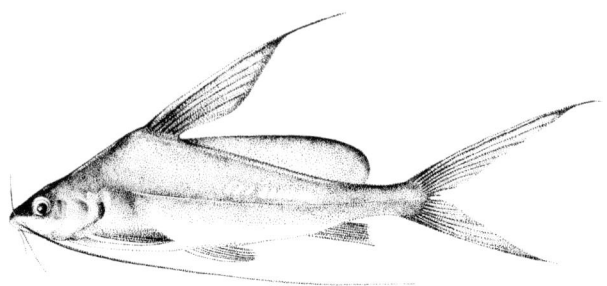

NOTES Maximum length 24 cm.

The body is dark grey or brownish grey, the belly brown; fins to match. An indistinct whiteish band may be seen slanting down the middle of each side.

Thailand : Pla kayeng wang

Cambodia : Trey chek tum

Vietnam : Cá chốt

Note the size of the dorsal fin and of the adipose fin behind it.

This species appears to be rare in Thailand, but is common in Laos. There are some other related species with different patterns of distribution, but none is of great importance.

CUISINE This relatively small catfish may be grilled or made into Mok pa. It is also used for padek.

*There is some doubt about the Lao name. Serène gave the name Pa sa gneng mo. Pa ka gneng po has been given to me as the name in the Vientiane market, Taki gives Pa katheung. Mr One Sy says that it is Pa gnon tung, tung meaning flag with reference to the large adipose fin (and being possibly equivalent to theung in katheung). Altogether, a puzzle.

Anyway, the fish of which the drawing appears above may be the wrong one! It was acquired as a specimen of **Bagroides macracanthus. However, the length of the maxillary barbels (which, according to Taki, should only extend back to the pectoral fins) suggests that it might really be a specimen of **Heterobagrus bocourti** (mentioned on page 72)). Oh well, wotthehell, as Archy would say to Mehitabel, even the frugal Lao don't eat the barbels and there's not much else to choose between the two species.

PA KHI HIA   ปา ฃึ่เฮี้ย   CATFISH

Leiocassis siamensis Regan

NOTES Maximum length 15 cm, common length about 12 cm.

The pattern shown in the drawing is typical, but subject to variation. The basic colour is black or dark brown, marked with white or light yellow. The fins are black or brown, except for the tail fin which is yellow marked with black.

Thailand : Pla kayeng hin,
         Pla kot hin

Cambodia : Trey kânchos thmâr

Vietnam : Cá chốt bông

The second Thai name is said to refer to the croaking sound (kot) which this fish makes, in the water and out of it. Fish of the genus **Mystus** (see next two pages) also have this habit, and many of them are also called Pla kot in Thailand.

CUISINE Small but good, with rich flesh. May be grilled or used in fish soups.

PA KOT   ປາ ກົດ   CATFISH

Mystus nemurus (C and V)
Macrones nemurus

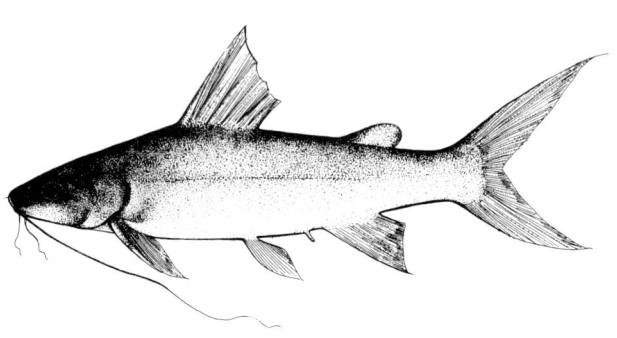

NOTES Maximum length 60 cm, usual length 35 to 40 cm.

    This is the largest of the numerous species in this genus. Colour varies with age and habitat. A typical specimen would have a brown body (lighter below) and perhaps a green sheen to it. The fins are grey; in adult fish they have brick-red edges.

Thailand : Pla kot,

Cambodia : Trey chhlaing (or chhlang)

Vietnam : Cá lăng

Other : Singgal (Indonesia); Ikan baung (Malay)

    Mystus wyckii (Bleeker) is another fairly large species (up to 45 cm); it is known as Pa kheung in Laos. It has a noticeably broad and flat head, upward-directed eyes, a violet back and white underparts.

CUISINE This is quite a good fish for frying or grilling. It may also be steamed according to the Lao recipes for Mok pa or Nung pa.

PA KA GNENG   ປາ ກະແຍງ   CATFISH

Mystus cavasius (Hamilton)
Mystus nigriceps
Macrones nigriceps

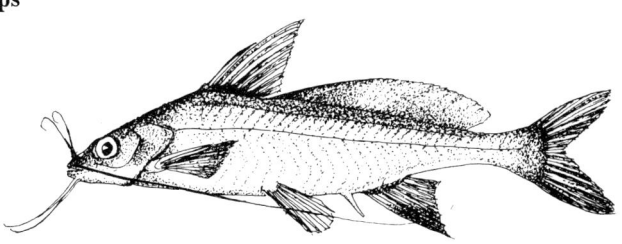

NOTES Maximum length 20 cm in Thailand and Laos (more in Indonesia and India).

The adult fish usually has a greenish or greyish brown back and sides and a white belly.

Thailand : Pla kayeng, Pla yeng*

Burma : (Nga-zin)

Cambodia : Trey kânchos chhnaut

Vietnam : Cá chốt là

Mystus rhegma (Fowler) and Mystus vittatus (Bloch) are two other species of about the same size, with dark bands running along their sides. It is not easy to distinguish them, nor is there any great point in doing so. Heterobagrus bocourti Bleeker deserves a mention here as a similar species which does, however, have a distinguishing feature in its very long dorsal fin, which sticks up almost as high as the fish is long. It is Pa ka gnen pho at Pakse and Pla kayeng tong in Thailand.

The Burmese name cited above is a general name which is applied to the various species of Mystus found in Burma. It may be enlarged to indicate a particular species, e.g. Nga-yaing-kyetchay for Mystus vittatus.

CUISINE   See preceding entry.

*The name Pla kayeng, or its shorter form Pla yeng, means ugly fish and is often applied to all the species of this genus. An interesting Thai name which applies to this and perhaps other species in some localities is Pla kayeng bai khau. Bai kha means rice leaf, which the adipose fin is thought to resemble by its shape and translucent light green colour.

PA KHE ປາ ແຂ້ CATFISH

Bagarius bagarius (Hamilton)

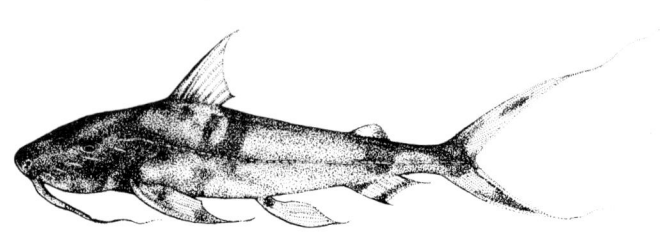

NOTES Maximum length is 2 metres. It is not uncommon to find specimens of 1 metre 10 or so in the Vientiane market, although most of those on sale are smaller.

A brown fish with darker markings and white dots along the lateral line.

Thailand : Pla kae, Pla kot kae

Burma : Nga-maun-ma

Cambodia : Trey krabey

Vietnam : Cá chên

This is a river fish and a voracious one. It gobbles smaller fish, frogs and shrimp. According to Prince Vipulya it likes to hide under logs and floating houses. The Lao and Thai names mean crocodile fish. The main fishing season is towards the end of the year, when the waters are subsiding after the floods.

The Pa khe has a depression on the top of its head. The Lao indicate the fish's size by saying that this hollow is 1, 2, 3 or 4 fingers across.

CUISINE A food fish of some importance in Laos; but it disagrees with some people. Others recoil from it because it looks like a ghekko, or because its flesh has an orange/yellow tint. Serène says that if sick people eat it they will become feverish. He also warns that the flesh rapidly spoils. Thus there are many reasons for treating the Pa khe warily.

In Luang Prabang they draw a distinction between specimens with yellow flesh (Pa khe leuam) and those with white (Pa khe khao). The former are preferred and are rated as very good material for padek.

3. PERCH-LIKE FISH

The order PERCOMORPHI is a very large one, including eight thousand or more species grouped in a large number of families, of which the family **Percidae**, consisting of the true perches, is only one.

The species of perch-like fish vary enormously in many respects, but they do have certain characteristics in common. The leading rays of the dorsal and anal fins are thick and stiff and often sharp. The pelvic fins too usually have a spiny ray, and lie well forward, under the pectoral fins. The pectoral fins are fairly high up on the body (not low-slung as in more primitive fish). The scales are usually ctenoid, that is to say with the free edge toothed.

From the galactic array of perch-like fish we have only eight species to consider here. The first three belong to the interesting family **Anabantidae**. Fish in this family possess an accessory respiratory organ, situated in a cavity above the gills, by means of which they can take oxygen directly from the air, through the mouth. In fact, although their gills enable them to breathe under water, like other fish, they must breathe air too and will suffocate if kept under water for long. The male fish blow air-bubbles which form little nests on the surface of the water for the reception and hatching of the female's eggs.

The remaining species in this section of the catalogue include the uncouth but delicious snakeheads, from the family **Ophicephalidae**; a triple-tail from the family **Lobotidae** (the same which includes well-known marine species); one representative of the family **Nandidae** and finally, one gody from the family **Eleotridae**.

PA KHENG ປາ ເຊັງ CLIMBING PERCH, WALKING FISH

Anabas testudineus (Bloch)

NOTES Maximum length 23 cm, common length 10 to 15 cm.

This is a brown fish, with a hard head and a tough, thick skin, which is famous for its ability to walk and even to climb. As for the climbing, Smith recalls the classic example :

Thailand : Pla mor, Pla sadet

Burma : Nga-bye-ma

Cambodia : Trey kranh

Vietnam : Cá rô dồng

Other : Betok (Indonesia); Pepuyu (Malay)

"In 1791 a Dane named Daldorff, while in Tranquedar, at that time a Danish possession in India, came upon a fish which, during a heavy rainfall, was climbing a Palmyra palm and had reached a point 5 feet above the ground. There it was apparently enjoying itself in a little stream running in a fissure in the palm's trunk from a broad frond which collected the rain water as in a funnel. Nearby was a swamp from which the fish had probably come."

This report was received with scepticism. Smith says that he does not himself doubt its accuracy. The fish was capable of climbing a Palmyra palm and could have been tempted to do so by the stream of water flowing down it. However, the occurrence was unusual. One does not often find a fish up a tree (although it happens in Cambodia that, when the waters subside in the forests which are flooded annually, some poor fish are caught in the upper branches of trees, whence fishermen can pluck them like fruit); and **Anabas** itself normally chooses to scale less dramatic heights. Drawing on his own experience in Thailand, Smith continues thus:

"The climbing powers of **Anabas** are exercised chiefly in leaving its home in a pond, swamp, or canal and seeking other water that may afford better living conditions. . . . In Siam, I not infrequently came upon an **Anabas**, usually at night, crossing a dusty road or traversing a dry lawn or field. It was easy to discover the water that a fish was leaving but it was not always possible to determine the particular water to which it was heading. In some cases the body of water to which the fish was obviously bound did not seem to the human observer to be more attractive than the water that had been left. The banks of drying canals and ponds, up which the fish has to climb, may be high and steep, and skill and patience may be required to negotiate them; but on arriving at a new body of water the fish may exercise much less care in descending, and I occasionally saw one, apparently deliberately, roll or fall down a steep bank and go into the water with a splash."

CUISINE An important food fish throughout S E Asia, but not of the finest quality. It is bony.

It may be grilled or used (in Laos) for Ponne pa (page 157). See also the recipe for Knap pa (second version) on page 128; and Lap pa kheng on page 135.

PA SA LIT   ປາ ສລິດ   SNAKESKIN GOURAMY

Trichogaster pectoralis (Regan)

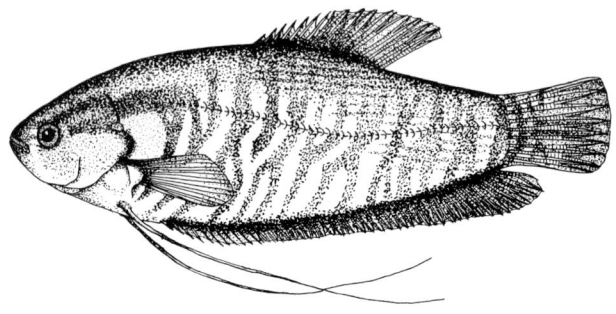

NOTES Maximum length over 20 cm, common length about 15 cm.

The basic colour is grey to brown, with greenish or bluish gleams. Note the blackish 'chain' along the side, the large pectoral fins and extended pelvic fins.

This fish lives in lakes, ponds and still or sluggish waters generally, feeding on aquatic plants.

Thailand : Pla salid, Pla bai mai

Burma :

Cambodia : Trey kantho

Vietnam : Cá sặt rằng

Other : Sepat Siam (Indonesia and Malay)

Trichogaster trichopterus (Pallas) is smaller and bears the Lao name Pa ka dout. It is Pla kadi mor in Thailand, and Trey kamphlieng samre in Cambodia. It is a dominant species in shallow stagnant waters.

CUISINE A fish of good quality. It may be grilled, or used for fish soup. In Thailand there is a trade in dried fish of this species, for the benefit of people living in areas where it is not caught.

PA MENG   ປາ ເຫຼັນມ   GOURAMY, GORAMY

Osphronemus goramy Lacépède

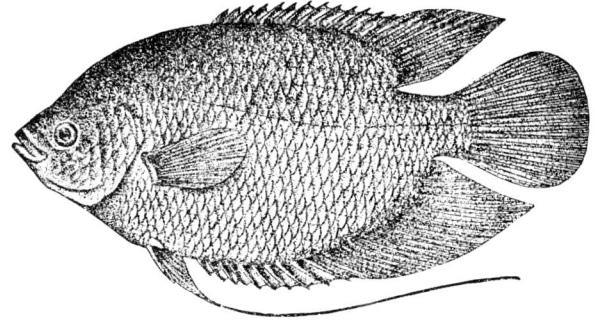

NOTES Maximum length 60 cm. Some of the largest specimens are said to be those in the ponds of certain Buddhist temples in Thailand, which may weigh 10 kilos.

Thailand : Pla raet, Pla min

Cambodia : Trey romeas

Vietnam : Cá tai tượng

This species may have originated in the East India islands, but has long since become naturalised in Thailand, Indochina, China, India and elsewhere. The head and body are yellowish to chocolate, sometimes with greenish tints. The darker vertical bands on the sides are irregular.

Maxwell recalls, in his book on Malayan Fishes, that he reared gourami, which he knew as kalui, in a pond at Kuala Pilah. "The Kalui in my pond were fed daily on leaves, principally wild caladium and tapioca shoots, not thrown broad-cast but inserted in split bamboo poles which were pushed into the bottom of the pond. They ate a tremendous lot and grew very rapidly; the caladium leaves imparting a very fine flavour to the fish. They will rise to a fly or beetle, and some flowers, particularly a large Hibiscus."

CUISINE The naturalist Commerson "stated that he never ate any fish more exquisite in flavour, whether from the sea or fresh water" (Day). However, Smith records that in Thailand the flesh was considered "of somewhat rank flavor". The Lao take a middle view, and the following is a Lao way of preparing the gouramy. Scale the fish, cut thin fillets off it lengthways and grill these very lightly, then use the fillets for Koy pa.

PA KHO ປາ ຄໍ້ SNAKEHEAD

Ophicephalus striatus   Bloch
Channa striata

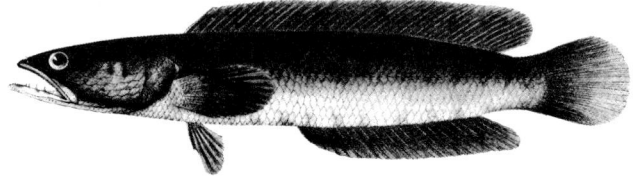

NOTES Maximum length about 1 metre, common length 30 to 70 cm.

The male (shown in the drawing) is almost black, with a hint of green, above; the female is less dark and has a more rounded head.

This species has a wide distribution, from India and Ceylon to Indonesia, the Philippines and China. It is one of the fish which survive the dry season by sinking themselves into the bottom mud of lakes, canals and swamps. As long as the skin and breathing apparatus remain moist the fish can live thus, subsisting on its stored fat for months on end until the rains start again. Fishermen cut the mud away with long knives, searching for the cavitiies, which may be almost a metre below the surface, in which the fish are hidden. (Any muddy taste can be dispelled by keeping the fish in fresh water for a while before eating them.)

Thailand :   Pla chon (chorn)

Burma :   Nga-yan

Cambodia :   Trey ros (or ras)

Vietnam :   Cá lóc

Other :   Aruan, Toman (Malay)

CUISINE This is perhaps the main food fish in Thailand, and of great importance in Laos. the rest of Indochina and Malaya. The flesh is firm, white and almost bone-free. Smith found the flavour suggestive of the American black bass.

Fishmongers usually cut the heavy dark skin off the body before selling it. The head makes a good soup and is usually sold separately.

PA DO ปา โด SNAKEHEAD

Ophicephalus micropeltes (C and V)

NOTES Maximum length about 1 metre, usual length 30 to 70 cm.

The colour is similar to that of the preceding species, but there are no stripes on the lower part of the body of adult specimens, and the upper part may be blotched. Small specimens bear very bold black and white lateral stripes which give them a distinctive appearance.

Thailand : Pla chado, Pla melang pu

Cambodia : Trey chhdor (diep for small ones)

Vietnam : Cá bông

Other : Toman (Indonesia and Malay)

This fish (and, I assume, the preceding species) has an unpleasant character. According to Hellei it attacks isolated Khmer fishermen. Worse, it is one of the few fish which devour their own young, at least in certain circumstances. Maxwell explains that the parents protect their offspring to begin with but then, when the little ones are big enough to fend for themselves, drive them from the nest. It is those which are too obstinate to leave which are eaten. The Malays have a saying: "Bagai toman makan anak". This means "like the Toman fish which eats its own young"; the phrase is applied to persons in high places who misuse their powers, oppressing those whom they should protect.

CUISINE Some say that this is not quite as good as the preceding species; but it is still of high quality. The firmness of the flesh makes all the snakeheads suitable for fish salads and cold fish dishes.

PA KANG ປາ ກັ້ງ SNAKEHEAD

Ophicephalus gachua Hamilton

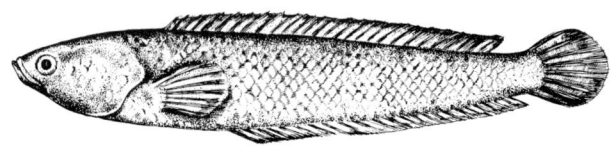

NOTES This, the smallest of the snakeheads, has a maximum length of 20 cm and is adapted to living in mountain streams.

The body is black, especially on the upper parts, and the fins are

Thailand : Pla kang

Burma : Nga-yan-gaungdo

Vietnam : Cá chành dục

black too; but the dorsal and tail fins have thin blood - red edges. The pectoral fins bear black cross - bands which may explain the Lao name (kan means striped or patterned).

Ophicephalus lucius C and V is a larger species, but at a maximum length of about 40 cm it is still much smaller than the two best-known snakeheads, which appear on the preceding pages. It is brown above and yellowish below, with darker spots and zigzags. Of the various snakeheads this one has the most snake-like head. Its range extends to Indonesia and China.

CUISINE See the preceding entries.

PA SEUA   ปา เสือ   TRIPLETAIL

Datnioides microlepis Bleeker

NOTES Maximum length 40 cm, common length 20 cm.

The basic colour of the fish is pale, be it pale cream, pink, yellow, greenish yellow or buff (depending on the habitat). It is on this background that the bold chocolate or black bands stand out. Specimens in Borneo and Sumatra have 7 such bands, those on the Asian mainland only 6, as shown in the drawing. The fins are light brown, but the membranes of the spiny dorsal and pelvic fins are blackish.

Thailand : Pla seua taw

Cambodia : Trey kla

Vietnam : Cá hường vện

The Lao, Thai and Cambodian names all mean tiger fish.

In fine weather this fish will often come up to the surface of the water and remain there, motionless. A Lao fisherman may then shoot it with an arrow.

CUISINE An excellent food fish. In Thailand it is said that the fisherman quickly sells his catch locally and few specimens reach the market. The fish is moderately popular in Laos. It is used for Lap pa; but it may also be grilled.

PA KA   ปา ก่า   STRIPED NANDA

Pristolepis fasciatus (Bleeker)

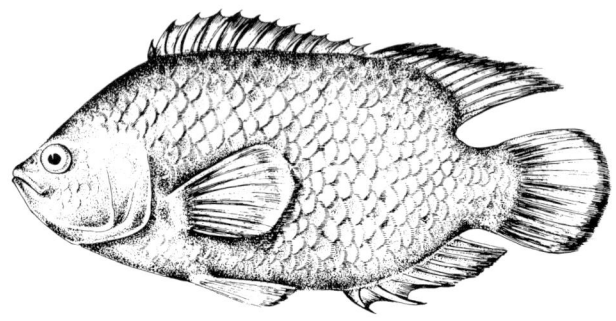

NOTES Maximum length 20 cm.

The general colour is greenish brown or brownish yellow. Most specimens are marked by 8 to 12 dark vertical bands. The fins are brownish or greenish.

Thailand : Pla mor chang yieb, Pla patong

Cambodia : Trey kantrâp

Vietnam : Cá rô thia

The body is thin. Prince Vipulya wrote: "It digs down into the mud of stagnant ponds and on account of its flat appearance is supposed to have been trodden on by elephants going to bathe. Hence the name."

CUISINE The flesh is bony, but has a good flavour. In Thailand it is esteemed less than the climbing perch (page 74) to which it bears some resemblance.

| PA NIN | ປາ ນິນ | TILAPIA |

Tilapia nilotica (Linnaeus)

NOTES Maximum length about 35 cm, corresponding to a weight of about 2½ kilos.

Thailand :

Vietnam : (Cá phi)

Tilapia are African fish of the family **Cichlidae**, and may have been cultured by the Egyptians more than 4000 years ago. More recently, they have been cultured in East Africa and in parts of Asia. Several species of the genus have been tried out in Laos, including **Tilapia mossambica**, but the experts have found that **Tilapia nilotica** is the best, since it grows faster than the others and reaches a larger size.

This species has a silver-grey body marked by 9 or 10 vertical bars on the body and little ones on the tail. The tips of the fins and tail are sometimes reddish. The scales are small.

The habits of the species are agreeable. It is herbivorous. The male has the task of making a nest in the soft bottom of a pond or stream. He must then swim round this, looking attractive, until a female is lured to lay eggs in it. Once the male has fertilised the eggs they are kept in the female's mouth for a few days until they hatch.

CUISINE The flesh of the tilapia is good, and not too bony.

PA BOU ປາ ບູ່ GOBY

Oxyeleotris marmoratus (Bleeker)

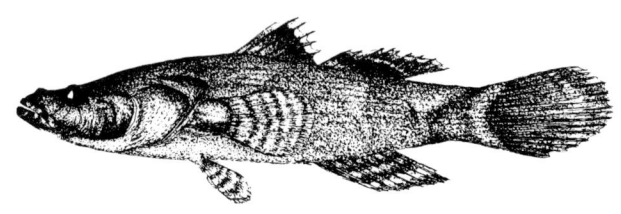

NOTES Maximum length 50 cm, and thus one of the largest gobies in the world.

The chocolate-brown colour accounts for the Cambodian name, which means elephant-fish.

This is another fish which can survive for quite a long time out of water. It is common in the Mekong and in swamps.

Thailand : Pla bu, Pla bu sai

Cambodia : Trey damrey

Vietnam : Cá bống

Other : Betutu (Indonesia)
Belontok (Malay)

CUISINE This is accounted the best of all freshwater fish in Cambodia. Its relative rarity may contribute to this reputation and to its high market price.

The Chinese also think highly of it. It is the subject of fish culture at Singapore (and in Thailand too).

4. OTHER FISH, ETC

A MISCELLANEOUS COLLECTION

I conclude the catalogue by listing species which do not belong to any of the large groups dealt with so far.

The featherback, spiny eels and swamp eel are straightforward freshwater fish. But the last five species to be listed all belong to families which are primarily marine. They excite interest for this reason, seeming to be out of place at such a great distance from the sea.

Finally, it must be said that fish are not the only edible creatures in the waters of Laos. Some of the others, such as frogs and certain snakes, have no place in this book. But freshwater shrimp and crab and turtle require mention, if only because their marine counterparts are often grouped with sea-fish under the category of seafood.

The crabs of Laos are edible, but not especially good. I have not yet been able to find out what are the species, and have not listed them in the catalogue. I should, however, mention that they are used at Luang Prabang to make a particularly good kind of nam pa (fish sauce) and that I have been advised to try eating them raw with a papaya sauce.

The small freshwater shrimp and the soft-shelled turtle are both good to eat and find a place at the very end of the catalogue.

PA TONG   ปา ตอง   FEATHERBACK

Notopterus chitala (Hamilton)

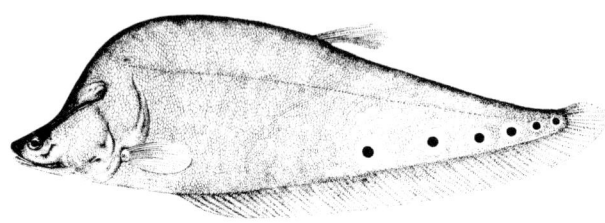

NOTES Maximum length 90 cm, or even 1 metre; normal length about 75 cm.

This is a thin and silvery fish with a distinctive head. It and its close relations are easily identified by the long anal fin and the small dorsal fin (like a feather in the back). The adults are marked by five to ten black spots in the position shown. (The young have dark vertical stripes which gradually fade away.)

Thailand : Pla krai, Pla hang pan
Burma : Nga-pe-gone
Cambodia : Trey kray
Vietnam : Cá còm
Other : Lopis (Indonesia); Belida (Malay); Chitala (Bengal)

The featherback lays eggs, usually on a stake or stump of wood. The male fish looks after these, fanning them with his tail to keep them aerated and free of sediment, and guarding them againts small catfish and minnows. "Fishermen sometimes take advantage of the male's devotion by fishing at a stake or stump which has been found to bear eggs....The female parent is never observed at the egg posts under circumstances that indicate maternal solicitude." (Smith)

CUISINE The featherbacks are moderately important food fishes throughout the region; but they have lots of small bones, especially in the back. However, if the flesh is finely grated or pounded, these disappear. (I have observed fishmongers in both Saigon and Phnom Penh scraping the flesh off for their customers and forming it into what look like fillets.) In Laos the featherbacks are favoured for the confection of Mok pa, Mok pa fok, Lap pa and Luk sin pa.

| PA TONG | ປາ ຕອງ | FEATHERBACK |

Notopterus notopterus (Pallas)

NOTES Maximum length 65 cm (in Laos; it seems to be less in Thailand, Indonesia etc). This species is similar to the preceding one, although the colour may be light bronze rather than silvery. Vertical stripes appear on young fish only.	**Thailand :** Pla chalat (salat) **Burma :** Nga-pe **Cambodia :** Trey slat **Vietnam :** Cá thát lát

Some authorities distinguish as a similar but separate species **Notopterus blanci** d'Aubenton, which bears on the rear part of its body a pattern of dark curving lines and spots (as shown in the second drawing); but others treat this fish as a variant of **Notopterus notopterus**.

All the featherbacks are fish of rivers, canals and swamps. They have a habit of coming to the surface of the water and rolling over with a splash. No doubt this antic has some purpose. The Thai name means cunning or clever fish.

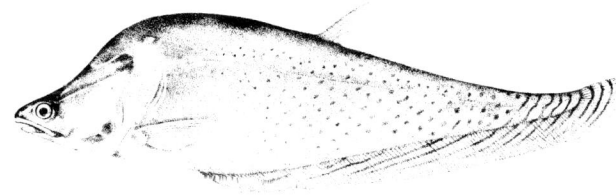

CUISINE This species is less good than **Notopterus chitala**. Its shape and smaller size make it suitable for being smoked whole.

PA LAT   ປາ ຫລາດ   SPINY EEL

Mastacembelus armatus favus Hora

NOTES This species, of Laos and Thailand, differs little except in colour from **Mastacembelus armatus armatus** Günther which has a range from India to Indonesia and the South of China. For practical purposes the two may be treated together.

The maximum length in Laos seems to be about 40 cm.

Thailand :   Pla kathing (bull fish)

Burma :   Nga-thinbawmo

Cambodia : Trey khchung (chhlaunh)

Vietnam :   Cá chạch lấu

Other :   Tilan (Malay)

This is a brown or yellowish brown fish, with darker brown or blackish markings. It looks like an eel, but differs from the true eels in having a spine of real bone. It is troublesome to handle; its short strong spines can inflict painful wounds.

The spiny eels are found in rivers, canals, swamps and lakes. Another spiny eel with a wide distribution in the region is **Macrognathus aculeatus** (Bloch), Pa lot in Laos and Pla lot in Thailand. It is slightly smaller, and brown or grey in colour, with a row of three eyelike marks along the base of the dorsal fin. See the drawing below.

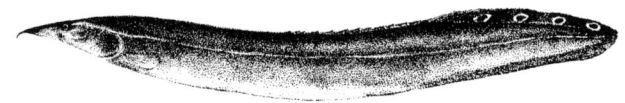

CUISINE Good eating, despite their appearance. Day and Hamilton noted the popularity of this fish in India and Bengal. The smaller ones may be pan-fried whole.

I'EN* or PA LAI   ອຽນ   PADDY EEL, SWAMP EEL

Fluta alba   (Zuiew)
Monopterus albus

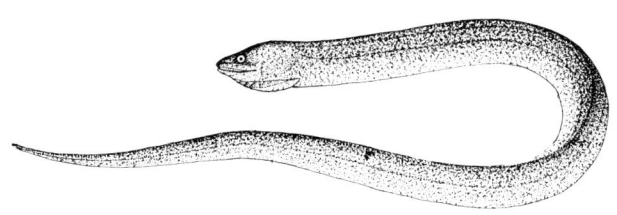

NOTES Some specimens may be nearly 1 metre long, but the common length is from 25 to 40 cm.

The back is greenish brown, the underside lighter.

A fish of ponds, swamps, canals and ricefields, widely distributed on the Asian continent and islands. When the dry season begins these fish bury themselves in the moist earth, whence they are dug up rather than fished. They will then survive for a long time out of water, provided that they are kept moist.

Thailand :   Pla lai**
Cambodia .   Antong
Vietnam :   Con lươn
Other :   Belut (Malay)

CUISINE The flesh is good and may be prepared in various ways. In Laos it may be used for Or pa or in the unusual dish called Lam i'en (page 132). Another Lao technique is to clean the fish and then beat it with the flat blade of a cleaver so as partly to flatten it and incidentally loosen the flesh from the bone. Sections of the fish thus treated are then gripped in cleft pieces of bamboo and roasted over a charcoal fire.

*Usually transcribed as Yen, but I'en is better (the sound is very close to the name Ian).
The prefix Pa is not normally used with this name.
**The general Thai name for eels.

PA FA LAI ປາ ຝາໄລ STING-RAY

Dasyatis sp.

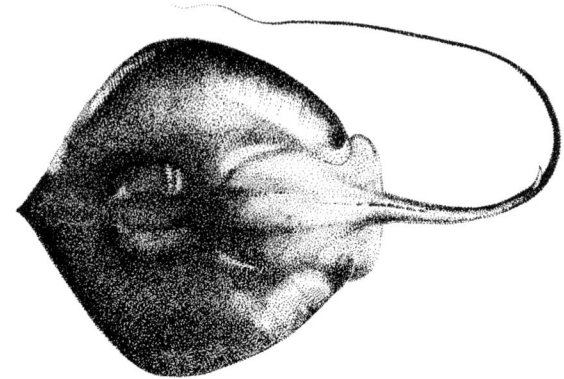

NOTES Maximum length (of the body only) 40 cm.

A species of sting-ray is found up and down the Mekong in Laos, but there is evidently some uncertainty about which it is.

Thailand : Pla kaben, pla ben

Cambodia : (Trey pabel)

Vietnam : (Cá đuôi)

Sting-rays are normally marine fish, some of which enter fresh or brackish water; but this one has made its home exclusively in fresh water. It attracts attention in some markets because of its unusual appearance, but is well-known at Luang Prabang.

In handling this sting-ray it is necessary to avoid being pricked by the poisonous tail-spines. Serène states that some Lao fishermen have died from wounds; and that the traditional remedy is to apply a plaster of sugar to the affected part. (The usual procedure is to cut off the spine as soon as the fish is caught. Serène further explains that the spine is an important item of witchcraft and that it is, for example, often worn by women in their hair as a prophylactic against the Phi pop, or malign spirit.)

CUISINE The stingray is regarded as quite good eating at Luang Prabang. It is often presented in the market in ready-cut pieces rather than whole. These are used for making Mok pa, as explained in the admirable recipe of Phia Sing which appears on page 144. Note that there are two little 'balls' of succulent flesh in the head area.

PA PE ປາ ແປະ SOLE

Synaptura harmandi Sauvage

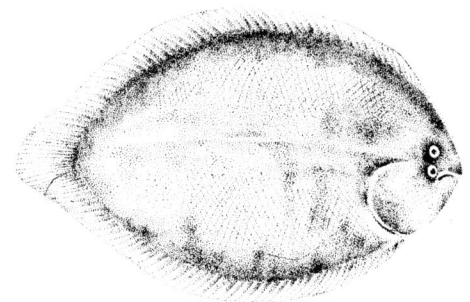

NOTES Maximum length about 15 cm. This is the only flatfish found in Laos. Its upper side is brown, with dark brown blotches; its underside white to pale brown.

Thailand : Pla lin kwai, Pla lin ma*

Cambodia : (Trey andat chhké)

Most flatfish are marine, and only some of them are willing to enter brackish or fresh water. There are, however, in South East Asia several species which have established themselves in fresh water far from the sea; and this is one of them. A specimen was first collected from the Mekong by Harmand; hence the specific name chosen by Sauvage.

"There is a deep-seated and widespread belief in Thailand that the soles of the genera **Synaptura** and **Cynoglossus** attach themselves to the bottom of boats and there make musical sounds. This belief persists from generation to generation and loses little strength with the passage of the years, notwithstanding that no one has ever seen a sole attached to either a stationary or a moving boat, and no one has ever observed the fish while making musical or other sounds either in or out of the water." (Smith)

CUISINE It is unnecessary to make suggestions for cooking a sole. But I should point out that this is rather a small sole and that its flavour is inferior to that of fine soles of the sea.

*Lin means tongue, kwai water-buffalo and ma dog. Thus the second name is a perfect match for the scientific name of the genus **Cynoglossus**.

PA MAK PHANG   ປາ ຫມາກຜາງ   HERRING

Hilsa kanagurta (Bleeker)
Clupea kanagurta

NOTES Maximum length 17 cm.

The presence of this species, which is well-known as a marine fish from East Africa to Indonesia, in the Mekong and its affluents is surprising. Smith stated that it does not habitually ascend streams; yet here it is, having apparently made its home in rivers 2000 kilometres from the sea.

Thailand : Pla mong kroi
Cambodia : Trey palung
Vietnam : Cá mòi dầu
Other

In appearance it has the typical shape of the herring family. The body is silvery-grey with a round black blotch on the shoulder (the only survivor of a row of four or five which appear on young specimens). Mak pang in the Lao name refers to a fruit which is bright yellow in colour and sour in taste, which comes into season in December.

There is at least one other freshwater herring in the region, **Clupea thibeaudeaui** Durand, the Trey kébâk of Cambodia.

CUISINE This fish may of course be treated according to any standard recipes for the herring or shad which it resembles. If like myself, you take care to be provided with oatmeal wherever you go in the world, you will be able to split open a Pa mak pang, coat it with oatmeal and fry it thus in the Scots fashion.

The Lao regard this fish as especially suitable for being grilled. In the south of Laos it is used for **Pa chao (page 149)**.

| PA SA THONG | ປາ ສະທົງ | GARFISH |

Xenentodon canciloides (Bleeker)

NOTES Maximum length 28 cm.	**Thailand :** Pla katung heo
This species is easily recognised by its long beak. The body is pale brown or whiteish, with an iridescent lustre, and bears a silvery stripe from gill opening to tail.	**Burma :** Nga-phoung-yoc
	Cambodia : Trey phtoung
	Vietnam : Cá nhái

The garfish are predominantly marine species; but those of the genus **Xenentodon** are found in fresh water only, from India to Indonesia.

The Lao name has an interesting explanation. Sa thong is a long piece of banana stem which, suitably decorated, is placed in front of a Lao house during the annual celebrations of the Buddha's birth. I have heard it said that the beak of the garfish is thought to resemble this. But Mr One Sy points out that this same piece of banana stem is used to float candles down the river, and that the garfish is a surface swimmer; so there is a further point to the name. Incidentally, in the south of Laos the name Pa katung (like the Thai name) is used.

CUISINE This is a good fish, like its larger cousin in Atlantic and Mediterranean waters. Bone-free fillets may be cut from it easily, although it is rather finicky work with the smaller specimens (which can always be used for fish soup).

PA KOUANG ປາ ກວາງ DRUM, CROAKER

Pseudosciaena soldado (Lacépède)

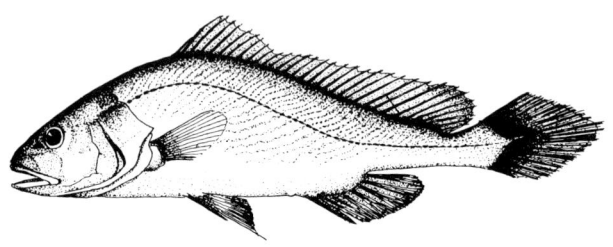

NOTES Maximum length 45 cm.

Thailand : Pla ma

This is another curiosity. The family **Sciaenidae**, a large group of fish collectively known as drums or croakers, is basically a marine one. Yet this one species is found as far up the Mekong as Luang Prabang, besides being abundant in the Tonle Sap in Cambodia.

Cambodia : Trey pama

Vietnam : Cá sửu

It is a light brown fish, with a greenish or greyish tint, with obscure ripple markings over the upper side of the body and a lighter underside. The fins are pale brown to yellow, but the tail fin is blackish and the spiny dorsal fin has a dark edge.

This fish is taken mainly in the dry season, during the period from January to April.

CUISINE This fish is sometimes available smoked, for example at Pak Cadinh and Paksane, downstream from Vientiane.

In Cambodia this fish is usually dried before being marketed.

| KOUNG | ກຸ້ງ | FRESHWATER SHRIMP |

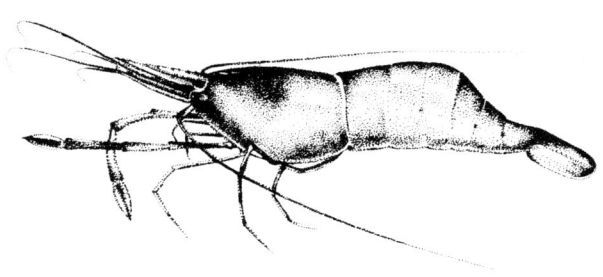

NOTES These little creatures are usually about 30 or 35 mm in length. They are grey/transparent in colour.

Thailand : Kung

Cambodia : Kampoes

CUISINE Here is a Lao way of consuming these small creatures while they are still alive.

Boil some crushed stalks of lemon grass and round aubergines (mak kheua) in water, adding a little nam padek after a while. If possible include a little chopped pork as well. When this stock is ready (after about 15 or 20 minutes) discard the lemon grass and strain out the mak kheua and the pork.

Sear and pound some onion, garlic and dried chilli pepper, incorporating also the pork and the mak kheua. Put the pounded mixture back in the stock. The shrimp (which have in the meantime been peeled alive) are now added to the stock with finely sliced spring onions and chopped mint; and the dish is ready.

PA FA ONG ປາ ຝາອອງ FRESHWATER TURTLE

Trionyx cartilagineus Boddaert

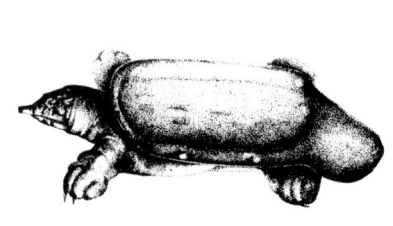

NOTES There are many different species of freshwater turtle in S E Asia. Bourret's admirable monograph covers the subject, but it is not always easy to know which species are found in Laos. The present species, which is one of those with a 'soft' or cartilaginous shell, is the most common in the markets; but hard-shelled aquatic turtles, possibly including the herbivorous **Batagur baska** Gray (whose eggs used to be reserved for the Queen Mother in Cambodia), are also offered for sale.

Thailand : Tapab nam

Cambodia : Kantheay

Trionyx cartilagineus grows to a fair size, but is best bought in fairly small editions (say 5 kilos) as the flesh is more tender. It is a carnivorous creature.

CUISINE This turtle is worth eating, although the Chinese have a strong preference for **Trionyx steindachneri** Siebenbock, which is a turtle of Tonkin rather than Laos. A mini-recipe for Tom som pa fa ong, a kind of Lao turtle soup, is given on page 165. I should add that a dignitary in Bangkok has assured me that ginseng goes particularly well with this turtle; and that it is beneficial for sore backs.

ODDITIES AND MYSTERIES

This is a book about edible fish. But whenever fish are discussed in Laos mention is likely to be made of various fish and other creatures which are renowned for other characteristics or are the subject of fabulous tales. Here are some notes on these oddities and mysteries.

FIGHTING FISH (PA KAT)

Thailand is famous for its fighting fish, of which there are several species. The best-known and most pugnacious is **Betta splendens** Regan, which is also found in Laos. It reaches a length of 5 cm in the wild state, but specimens bred in captivity will be larger and have even more fighting spirit. Smith has the following to say:

"In Siam, as in the various countries into which the fish has been introduced, the usual procedure in arranging a fight is to select two males of approximately the same size and bring them together in separate jars. If they spread their fins, show their colors, and make head-on efforts to reach each other, they are placed together in the same vessel . . . . The fish immediately approach each other and indulge in a preliminary display of spread fins, expanding gill membranes, and color waves. . . . Then, in quick succession, the fishes attack, their movements being so swift that the human eye can hardly follow the actual impact of the teeth, and the assaults are repeated with short intermissions, during which the same sparring attitude is taken.

"The most common points of attack are the anal, caudal, and dorsal fins. . . . The first evidence of a spirited encounter is likely to be torn or split fins. As the contest proceeds, there may be extensive loss of fin substance, and with well-matched fishes the vertical fins may ultimately be reduced to mere stubs.

"During the short interludes in fighting when the demand for oxygen forces the fishes to go to the surface for gulps of air, attacks are always suspended. I have never known one fish to assail another at such a time. It is literally a breathing spell provided for in the fighting fish's code of ethics.

"Fighting contests are decided by the general exhaustion and the failure of stamina in the combatants rather than by a definite injury or a knock-out assault. Sooner or later one fish shows a lack of ability or desire to continue the fight and swims away - literally turns tail - when his rival assumes a position for attack.

"At the end of a protracted contest both fishes may present a most unattractive appearance because of their mutilated fins, but they seem to experience no discomfort and, if permitted, would fight again the next day. The fins regenerate rapidly and completely, and at the end of a few weeks may show no signs of injury.

"My experience, which extended over 12 years and covered many hundreds of exhibitions, coincides with that of most observers in finding nothing brutal, cruel, or repulsive in fighting-fish contests. The participants seem to get so much satisfaction from their encounters, their physical discomfort is apparently so negligible, and their recovery is so complete that there is little occasion to expend sympathy over them, while their graceful movements, muscular agility, acumen, tenacity, and wonderful color displays cannot fail to arouse enthusiasm even in the most sensitive spectators."

ARCHERFISH (PA MEO)

The family **Toxotidae** includes several species of fish, all equipped with an astonishing ability to kill insects by propelling at them from their mouths, with a high velocity, small drops of water.

The species which occurs in Laos, although it is not common, is thought to be **Toxotes microlepis** (Günther). It is less widely distributed and less well-known than the famous **Toxotes jaculatrix**, which is **the** archerfish.

These fish are edible, but it is their shooting ability which makes them famous. During the 18th centuries it was doubted by scientists, but early in the present century the Russian ichthyologist Zlotinsky established the facts and thus described them:

"(1) The fish subsists largely on insects, which hover over the water or rest on overhanging vegetation. When a fish approaches within a certain distance of an insect, it becomes stationary, points its head and turns its eyes directly at the prey, brings the front of its mouth to the surface of the water, partly opens the mouth, and forthwith propels a drop, or several drops of water at the insect, which ordinarily is 12 to 20 inches distant, but may be 40 inches or more. The aim is true and the insect falls into the water and is at once devoured.

(2) The fish frequently swims backward. This habit is often observed when the fish reconnoiters a prospective prey, and backs from it in order to secure a good position for observation and attack.

(3) The eyes sparkle with seeming intelligence and their mobility is noteworthy. . . ."

The quotation is given by Smith, who goes on (page 494) to explain how the structure of the mouth of the archerfish enables it to practise dropshooting. He observes that marksmanship at moving insects is not nearly so accurate as against insects at rest, for example on overhanging vegetation, but that hits are often scored at distances well over 1 metre. "The force with which the watery pellets may strike an object is sometimes most astonishing to a human observer. An insect may be knocked high in the air or may fall on the bank beyond a fish's reach. At short range the drops may strike a person's face with a distinctly stinging sensation. . . . The shooting habit begins to develop early and may be observed in fishes only an inch long. It is most amusing to see the inexperienced youngsters emulating the actions of their parents and sending out tiny drops that may go only 2 or 3 inches."

PUFFER FISH (PA PAO)

At least two species of the Family **Tetraodontidae** are taken in Laotian waters. They belong to the same group as the well-known blowfish of Japan, which must be prepared with great care if he who dines on them is to enjoy their flesh without succumbing to the poison which some of their organs contain. The Lao, no doubt aware of the perils, do not eat these fish. Nor do they miss much thereby; for the species in Laos are small and relatively rare.

Lao children, however, used to use puffer fish as balloons, blowing them up by means of a straw through the mouth. Lip to lip blowing is dangerous because the puffer fish have two sharp teeth with which painful bites can be inflicted; whereby hangs another tale, told to me by Dr Pholsena. It seems that if you take a puffer fish, bite off its tail and put it back in the water, it will swim round in circles, waiting for the opportunity to revenge itself on the human species. If a nude bather comes near such a fish, the fish will attack the bather in a vulnerable place, usually the sexual parts. It used to happen in the South, when a courting couple quarrelled with sufficient bitterness, that the spurned lover would place such a de-tailed puffer fish in the pool where the erstwhile beloved was wont to bathe . . .

THE DUGONG (PA KHA)

From the vicinity of Khong Island come stories of a creature like a mermaid, with breasts and a forked tail, which is found in the Mekong below the Falls of Khong. This is the Dugong, which is not a fish, but a mammal. It belongs to a family which is represented in other parts of the world, notably by the Manatee in the West Indies.

The tears of the the dugong, if they can be gathered, are thought to make a fine love potion; and the oil from its body is used to light lamps. I have not heard of its being eaten in Laos. However, it is, or used to be, eaten in Malaya; and the manatee, according to data collected by Simmonds (Curiosities of Food, London, 1859), is delicious, with white flesh like pork. But the same author had qualms about consuming the delicacy. "It appears horrible to chew and swallow the flesh of an animal which holds its young (it has never more than one at a litter) to its breast, which is formed exactly like that of a woman, with paws resembling human hands."

This sort of consideration is reinforced in Laos by the reputation which the dugong enjoys for protecting fishermen. I have had a vivid description of how, when a pirogue sinks, a score or more of dugongs will appear and form a circle round the crew as they flounder in the water. The dugongs utter wheezing sighs of concern and are evidently bent on protecting the men from possible attacks by large and predatory fish.

ELECTRIC EELS (OR RIVER SNAKES)

It is a popular belief at Vientiane that a large creature which might be described as an electric eel dwells in the Mekong and that many otherwise inexplicable deaths from drowning are caused by this creature stunning a bather with its electric discharge. On certain occasions the spirits of the island opposite Vientiane have offerings made to them, in the hope that they will restrain the creatures from making such attacks. However, these electric eels are apparently never caught (the explanation being that if they were to be entangled in a net they would bite their way through the rope).

RIVER DRAGONS

One hears of these. A report which reached me in 1974 spoke of a river dragon 3 metres long which was terrorising the inhabitants of a river village. Perhaps such stories are based on the presence in Laotian waters of crocodiles and water monitors. But it has also been suggested to me that they arise from the presence in the Mekong of enormous river serpents. I am told that in the vicinity of Salakoktan, on the outskirts of Vientiane, it is possible to see such creatures undulating about on that day of the year when the waters of the Mekong first begin to subside after the rainy season. Mr Laurent Le Ky Huong has observed this twice, once through binoculars. He was able to relate the size of the creatures to that of a pirogue which was about the same distance away. He estimated the length at 20 to 25 metres, and noticed a red band on the neck about 40 cm down from the head. The head was precisely like that of a 'couleuvre'. The testimony of other witnesses matches his. (And the description given has a certain resemblance to that of the Loch Ness monster.)

COOKERY

NOTES ON COOKERY AND INGREDIENTS

The Lao recipes which are given further on are presented in full detail. However, readers to whom some of the utensils or ingredients are unfamiliar will find the recipes easier to follow if they first read this illustrated introduction.

A Lao cook will normally use a CHARCOAL BRAZIER (picture on page 101), and will certainly have a PESTLE AND MORTAR (familiar to all) in constant use. She will also employ frequently a STEAMER, such as the apparatus pictured on the right; and a WOK, shown below. The wok is a versatile pan, found all over S E Asia as well as in China, where I believe it was first evolved. Its shape permits frying with the minimum quantity of oil, while requiring the cook to move things around inside it to ensure even cooking.

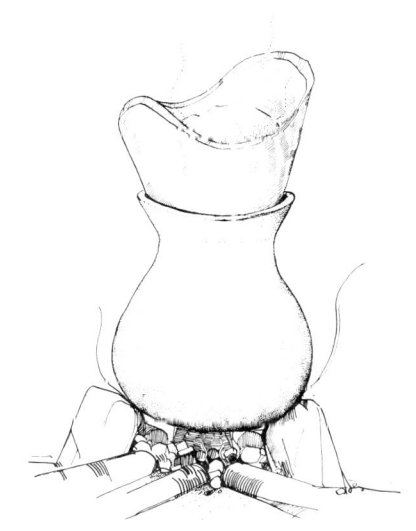

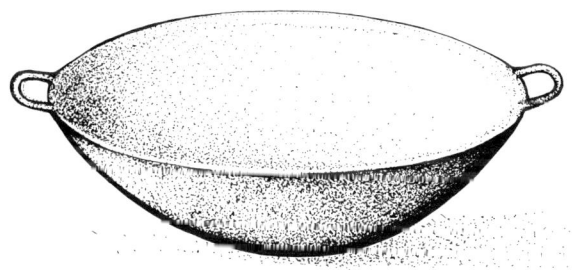

FISH SAUCE (NAM PA) is another ingredient which appears in almost every recipe. Every South East Asian country has its fish sauce (Nuoc mam in Vietnam, Tuk trey in Cambodia, Nam pla in Thailand, Ngan-pya-ye in Burma and so on). They are prepared by steeping fish in brine for a long time (a mixture of 20% sea fish and 80% freshwater fish is used in Laos) and draining off the liquor which is formed. It is brown in colour, rather like a peaty Scotch whisky, and comes either in a bottle or a stoneware jar.

PADEK is a related product, but in it chunks of the fish survive, so that it is necessary when using padek to know whether it is these chunks which are to be used or the liquor (nam padek) or both. Padek is made at home and kept in the sort of large earthenware jar which is illustrated. I am told that the Lao bride of a Westerner, offered tinned anchovies for the first time, exclaimed "But this is padek; rather salty padek, but good!"

MSG. This ubiquitous ingredient is monosodium glutamate, which recently enjoyed a vogue in the United States and Europe, under names such as Accent. I am told that questions have now been raised about whether it is good for one. However, people in South East Asia have used it enthusiastically for a very long time indeed as an agent which elicits from other ingredients the full strength of their flavour.

COCONUT CREAM

The liquid which you can hear slopping about inside a coconut before it is opened is known as coconut water or coconut juice. It is normally used for the preparation of soft drinks rather than in cooking. Coconut cream (or coconut milk - the terms are in practice interchangeable) is produced by taking out the white flesh of the coconut, grating it, adding water and then squeezing the mixture through a muslin or other suitable cloth. The process can be carried out twice with the same grated coconut. The first extraction will be thicker than the second; which is why one or the other is specified in the recipes.

Coconut cream may also be prepared from desiccated coconut, following the directions on the package. This is fortunate, because many South East Asian dishes depend for their distinctive flavour on coconut cream and could not otherwise be recreated in countries where fresh coconuts are unobtainable.

When cooking with coconut cream, be careful to keep stirring when the mixture is coming to the boil. Otherwise the coconut cream will curdle

RICE CAKES

These are mentioned in some recipes. Here is a drawing to show what they look like.

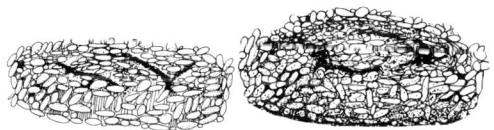

They are available ready-made in the markets (as KHAO KHOB) or may easily be made as follows. Cook some sticky rice in the ordinary way, then mould it into small cakes, let these dry and finally deep-fry them.

Cymbopogon nardus is the scientific name of CITRONELLA or LEMON GRASS, a plant which has the taste of lemon and is therefore often used in fish cookery. The Lao name is Bai mak nao. The usual procedure is to crush the stalks and then chop them, thus releasing fully the lemon flavour. The drawing of citronella is so beautiful that I have devoted the whole of the facing page to it.

The lemon itself is not available in Laos. As usual in tropical areas, the LIME, which is too well-known to require illustration, takes its place. But another member of the citrus family does require identification. This is **Citrus hystrix**, the KAFFIR LIME or PAPEDA, called Mak khi hout in Laos. Its leaves, broken into small pieces, are used in several Lao fish dishes.

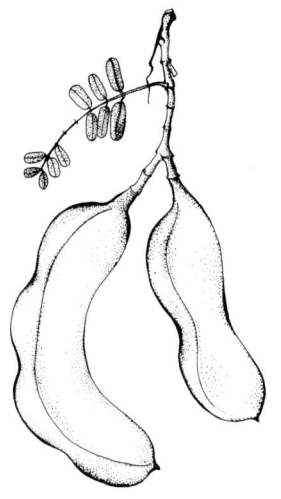

Another ingredient which gives an acid taste is the TAMARIND **Tamarindus indica**, of which both the pulp and the tiny leaves may be used. Its Lao name is Mak kham.

GINGER

The ginger plant, **Zingiber officinale**, is a native of Asia. The parts which are eaten are the irregular rhizomes (shown on the right) which form just below the surface of the soil. Fresh ginger is normally used in Lao dishes, cut in slices about as thick as a coin. The Lao name is Khing.

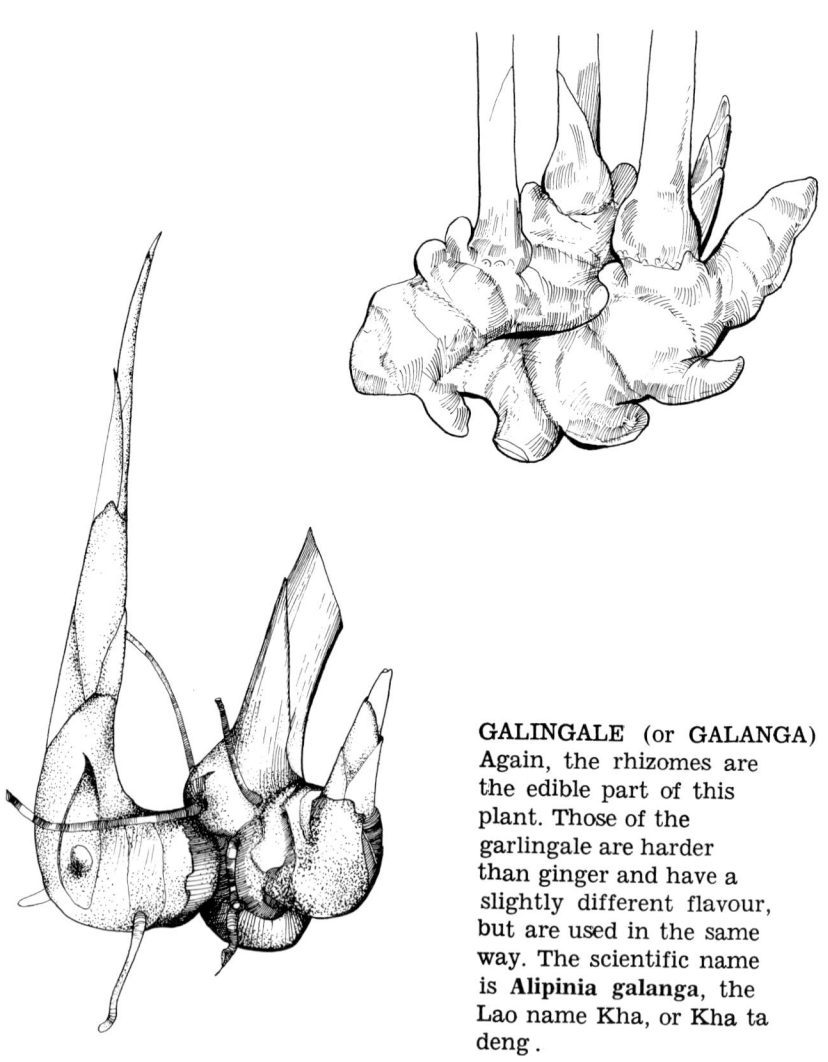

GALINGALE (or GALANGA) Again, the rhizomes are the edible part of this plant. Those of the garlingale are harder than ginger and have a slightly different flavour, but are used in the same way. The scientific name is **Alipinia galanga**, the Lao name Kha, or Kha ta deng.

The AUBERGINES or EGGPLANTS, **Solanum melongena**, are natives of Asia. The general Lao name for them is Mak kheua. The variety which is familiar in Europe and America - the one with the large, glossy, purple fruit - is nowadays available in Laos and is known as Mak kheua hamaa. But the Lao themselves use other varieties which are unfamiliar to Europeans and require illustration.

Mak kheua poy is the Lao name for a smaller, round eggplant, which is usually green in colour (but may also be white, yellow etc).

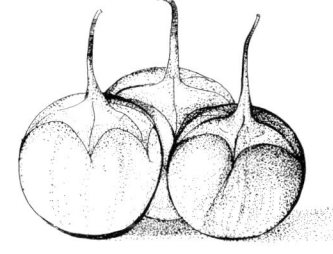

Mak kheng is the Lao name for another, much smaller variety. The fruits, which come in clusters and are green, are no bigger than small cherries or large peas. Mak kheng khom (not shown) is an even smaller variety which may be red in colour and has a very bitter taste.

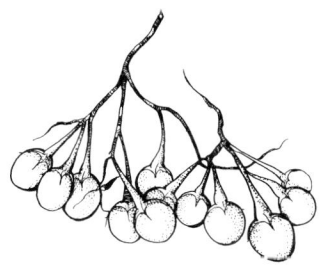

Mak thua nyao is the Lao name for the very long green beans shown below; **Vigna unguiculata**, sometimes known as the long-podded cow-bean or YARD-LONG BEAN (haricots baguette in French).

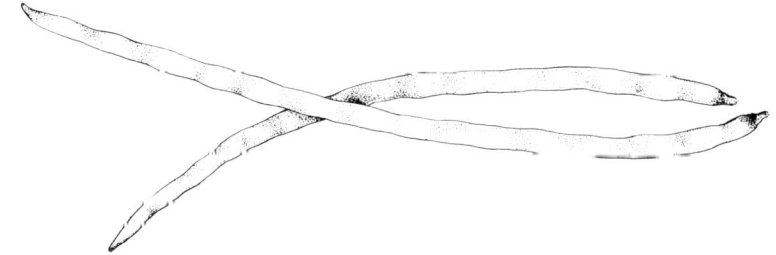

Allium cepa is the scientific name of various onion plants. The general Lao name for these is Phak boua. The common large ONION is known in Laos as **Phak boua nyai**.

SHALLOTS are used in most Lao fish dishes. The Lao name is Hom boua heng, or Phak boua houa pom, or Houa phak boua. Shallots are always sold dried, and have a purplish skin. The dried bulbs of spring onions (see next page), which are sometimes used in place of shallots, have a brown skin.

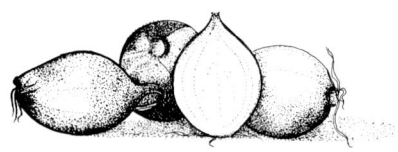

Allium sativum is the familiar garlic (Lao name Phak thiem). The heads of garlic grown in Laos are smaller than those of, say, France. The cloves are smaller too, and this is why Lao recipes often call for what seem like surprisingly large numbers of them. Garlic is of course almost always used in the form of dried heads; but sometimes a recipe calls for fresh garlic and for using the foliage.

A different sort of onion, which we know in the West as the SPRING ONION or SCALLION, is used in one way or another in most Lao fish dishes.

Spring onions are what you see growing outside almost all Lao houses, often on a little table raised on stilts.

The Lao name is Phak boua sot, or simply Phak boua. The leaves only are Bai phak boua; the head alone is Houa phak boua (whether fresh or dried).

All of the spring onion is edible, raw; but the part most commonly used is the green part, sliced across very thinly into tiny rondelles.

Bunches of the dried bulbs may be seen in the market. They are brown. They may be used, if necessary, as a substitute for shallots; but are usually sold for replanting.

A different variety of spring onion, which never develops a rounded bulb, is called Phak boua leui (or by the old-fashioned name Phak boua lai leung). It is well-known at Luang Prabang; and is cultivated mainly by the Kha and Lao Tung tribes.

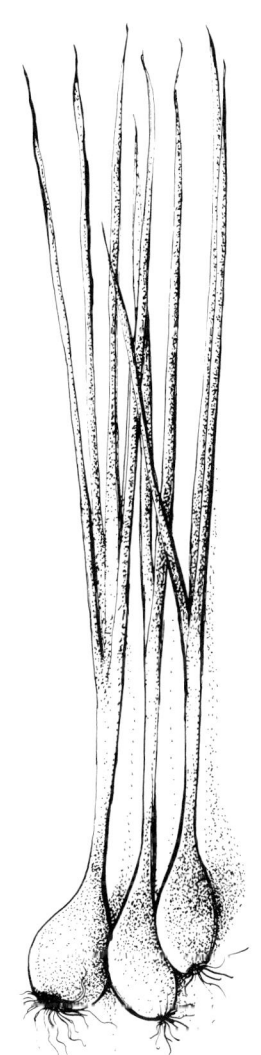

BEAN SPROUTS

These are grown from mung beans and may be bought fresh or tinned. The Lao name is Mak thua ngork.

PEPPERS

The word pepper has various meanings and is a frequent source of confusion (compounded by the practice of referring to green peppers and red peppers as though these were two different kinds, when the fact is that all pepper fruits are green when unripe and red or orange when ripe). What follows is intended to dispel the confusion.

Capsicum annuum bears a large fruit, which may be of various shapes (such as the bell pepper illustrated) but which is never very hot. It may be called GREEN PEPPER or SWEET PEPPER, or PIMIENTO. The Lao name is Phik.

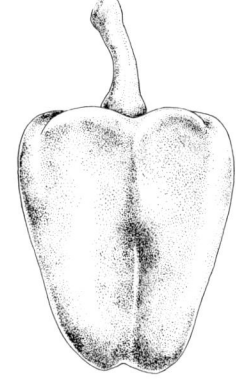

Capsicum frutescens is a perennial plant, bearing smaller fruit, bright red when ripe and much more pungent than the sweet pepper. They come in three sizes. Mak phet nyai are the largest. Mak phet kuntsi are small; and Mak phet kinou are really tiny ones. (Kinou is the Lao word for rat droppings, which these tiny peppers resemble in shape and size.) I call them all CHILLI PEPPERS, although some prefer to reserve the term chilli for the smaller sizes.

They are to be used with caution. The larger ones are a lovely pale jade green when marketed fresh and young. At this stage they are much less hot than later on. They are often dried when red and may then be used, after a soaking in water, for adding pungency and red colouring to Lao dishes. In the dried form they are called Mak phet heng.

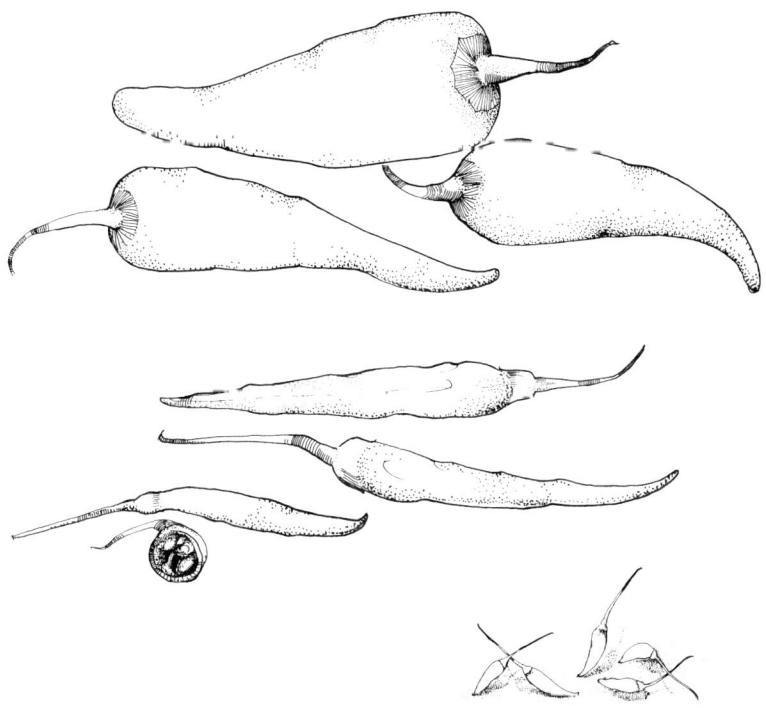

Piper nigrum (not shown) is something yet again - a kind of vine which bears the small fruit which we know as peppercorns. BLACK PEPPER is made from unripe peppercorns, WHITE PEPPER from ripe ones. The Lao name is Phik noi or Phik thai.

Petroselinum crispum, PARSLEY, FRENCH PARSLEY

This is plain parsley, familiar to all Europeans. The variety available in Laos is often that known as 'French' - it does not have the tightly curled leaves of the variety which is best known in Britain. It is not sold or used by the Lao, but may be had from Vietnamese greengrocers.

Coriandrum sativum

'CHINESE PARSLEY', CORIANDER

Coriander seeds are one thing. The leaves of young coriander plants are another. They are what are sold in Laos as 'Chinese parsley', and they have a very strong taste, beloved by most Lao but not by most Europeans. The Lao name is Phak hom pom.*

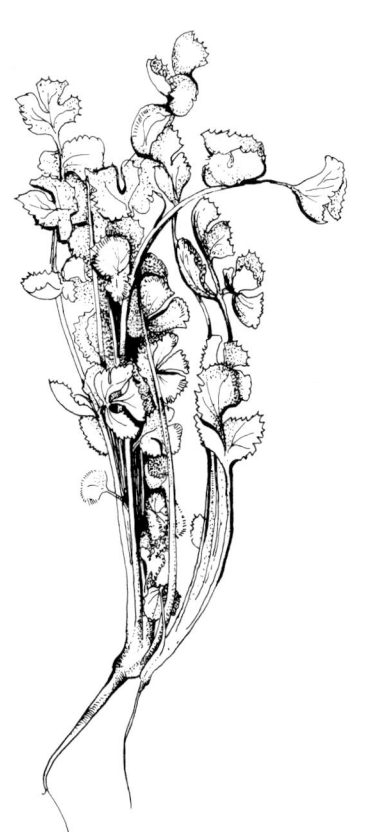

*NOTE The name Phak hom, sometimes shortened to Hom, may cause confusion. It is a general name for aromatic herbs and is to be interpreted according to the context as meaning mint, Chinese parsley, spring onion, dill, basil etc or a mixture thereof.

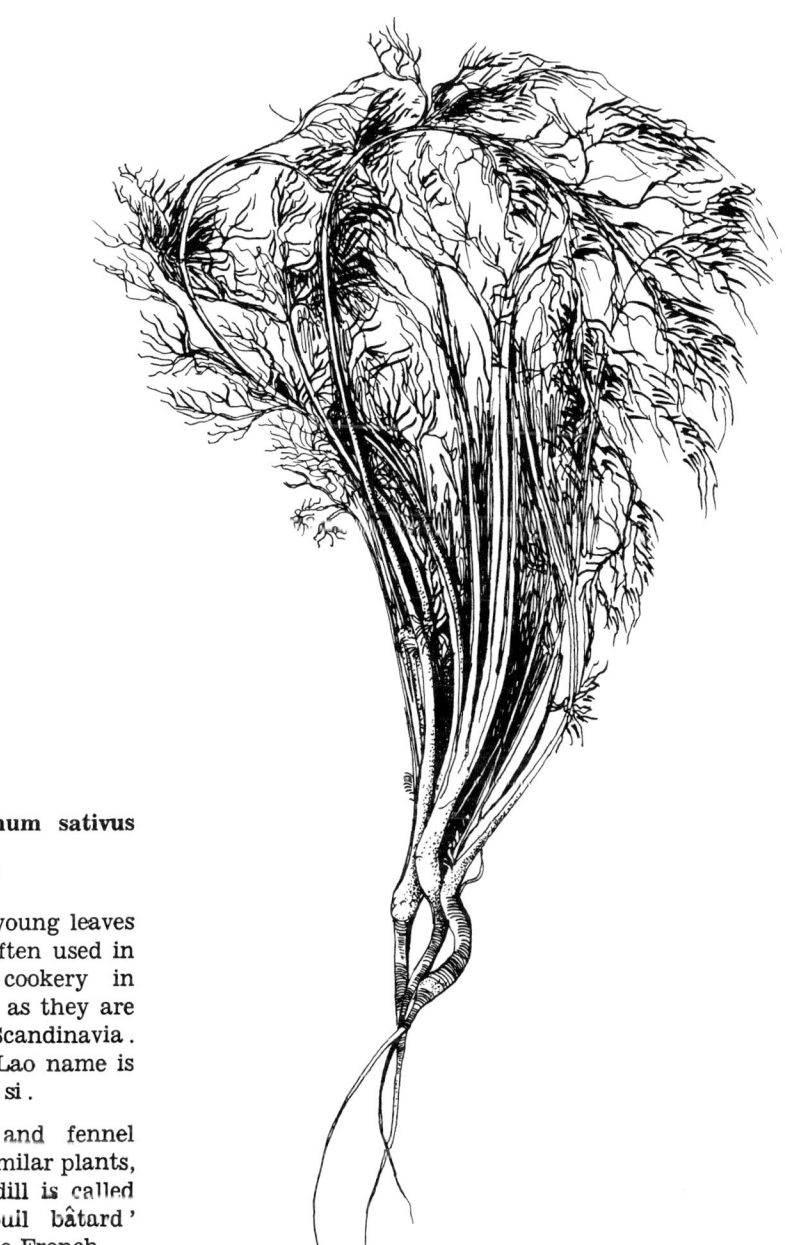

Anethum sativus

DILL

The young leaves are often used in fish cookery in Laos, as they are in Scandinavia. The Lao name is Phak si.

Dill and fennel are similar plants, and dill is called 'fenouil bâtard' by the French.

MINT and BASIL

MINT plays quite an important part in Lao fish cookery; and at least two kinds of mint grow in Laos. Lao names denoting mint are Phak hom ho; Phak kankam (kan means stalk, kam means darkish); and, in the South, Phak seum. One of the sorts of mint available appears to be of **Mentha sp.**, and very close to the mint which the English use for mint sauce. This is shown in the top drawing. The other mint which is commonly available is probably a sort of mint-leaved basil, **Ocimum menthaefolium**, but I have not been able to establish this definitely.

What is certain is that the genus **Ocimum** does provide other plants which are often used by Lao cooks. **Ocimum basilicum**, SWEET BASIL, is known as Phak itu lao and is shown in the drawing below centre. **Ocimum gratissimum**, shown below right, is called Phak boua la pha. It may also be called Phak itu thai, as may its close relation **Ocimum sanctum**, shown below left.

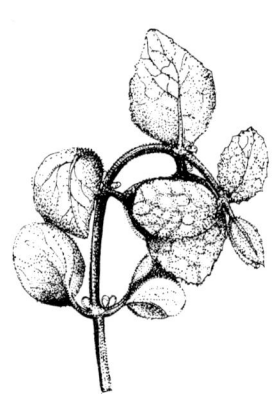

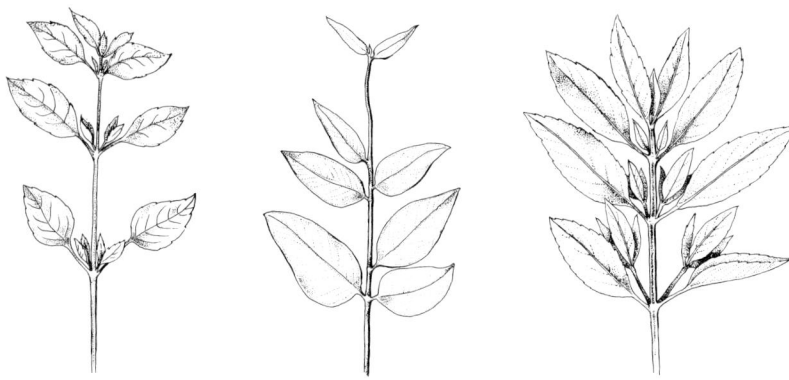

SALAD LEAVES

The familiar lettuce, Phak salat, is often used to provide leaves for wrapping up morsels of food before eating them.

Other salad leaves commonly used for the same purpose are those of **Brassica** sp., what would be called plain 'greens' in England. They are Phak kat khao in Laos. See the upper drawing.

Phak kat kieo, also of **Brassica** sp., have a different taste and correspond rather to mustard greens'

Another popular salad leaf, of **Piper** sp., is known as Phak i leut and is shown in the lower drawing.

OTHER EDIBLE LEAVES

There are many other edible leaves in Laos. In these two pages I provide illustrations of a few of those most commonly used.

Melothria heterophylla, Phak tam nin (or, say some, tam ling) is shown on the right.

Below is **Eryngium foetidum**, Phak hom thet.

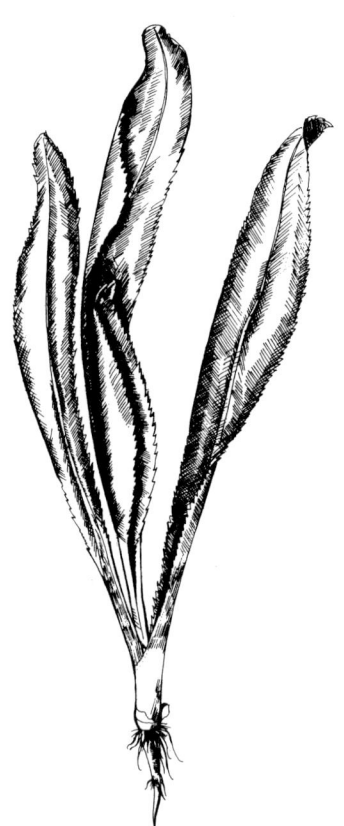

Polygonum odoratum, Phak pheo

Careya sphaerica, Phak kadone (a name also given to **Barringtonia sp.**)

Marsilea quadrifolia, Phak **wen**, is a plant of the ricefields.

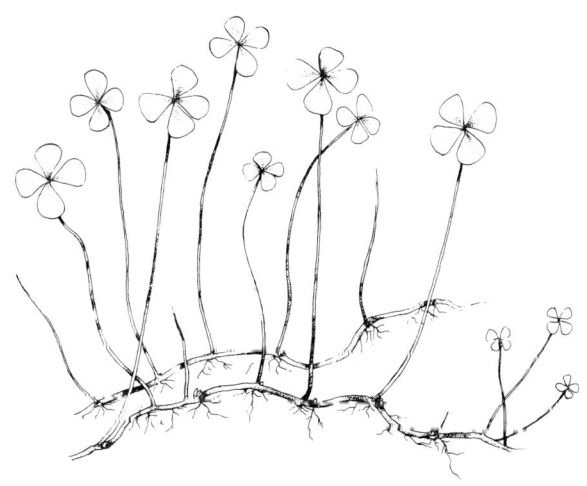

I hope that what I have said above about various ingredients will be sufficient to enable foreigners in Laos to find what they need to follow the recipes.

I have not adapted the recipes in any way for use outside S E Asia. Apart from any other considerations, there is so little published material available about Lao cookery that it seemed to me preferable to set down what I could find out as fully and accurately as possible, and without making changes.

Although there is a lack of published material, I should explain that there does exist one comprehensive set of Lao recipes, presented in an admirable manner. The late royal chef at Luang Prabang, Phia Sing, was an extraordinarily versatile man, a sort of Lao Leonardo who combined the skills of doctor, architect, choreographer, sculptor, painter, poet, master of royal ceremonies and chef. He set down in two little cahiers, such as schoolchildren use, the Lao recipes which were in his repertoire; all in beautiful Lao script and methodically organised by number. These precious volumes are of unique importance in their field. Thanks to the kindness of HRH The Crown Prince and Mme Phia Sing, I have had the loan of them for use in connection with this book and have permission to publish certain of the fish recipes from the collection. The reader will see for himself that these recipes (which are presented in a straightforward translation, with only the occasional addition, in square brackets, of additional information or instructions) are of exceptional quality. A photocopy of the entire collection has been deposited in the Bibliothèque Nationale at Vientiane, where it is available for future research workers on Lao foods and Lao cookery; and it is my hope that the Cahiers may be published in the near future, with an English translation and explanatory notes.

The Lao recipes are presented in alphabetical order of title, and are followed by a small selection of similar recipes from neighbouring countries.

LAO RECIPES

GNU MAK KHEUA

Fish with eggplant and beansprouts

1 kilo (cleaned weight) fish, preferably Pa khao (page 52) or other catfish
3 to 5 large eggplants (mak kheua)
2 soupspoonfuls vegetable oil
5 cloves garlic
5 shallots
3 soupspoonfuls nam pa (fish sauce)
1 teaspoonful MSG
½ cup chopped spring onions
½ cup fresh beansprouts (if fresh ones are not available omit this ingredient or change the menu)

Roast or grill the fish until it is cooked through, then pick out the bones. Roast or grill the eggplants and chop them finely.

Crush the cloves of garlic. Chop the shallots.

Pound the chopped eggplants for a few minutes in a mortar, then add the flesh of the fish and keep on pounding until you have all thoroughly mixed.

Heat the vegetable oil in a wok and brown the garlic and shallots therein. Add the fish and eggplant mixture and stir-fry for 5 to 8 minutes. Add the nam pa and MSG and continue for 5 more minutes; then the spring onions and beansprouts and again about 5 to 8 minutes' stir-frying, after which the dish will be ready to serve.

As usual, a number of variations may be applied to the recipe. One is to add mint leaves or Chinese parsley, or both, to the platter for decoration and additional taste when serving the dish. Another is to introduce 1 or 2 teaspoonfuls of powdered red pepper to the mixture while it is being cooked; an addition which may conveniently be made when you put the nam pa and MSG in.

(Nang Pheng of Ban Na Sai)

KENG PA SAY

Clear fish soup, as served at the Royal Palace

Ingredients

pork bones (dook moo)
1 fish, grilled and deboned
1 small bowl of shallots
a piece of keuak kwai (the roof of the mouth of a water-buffalo), boiled and sliced
2 hen eggs, hard-boiled and sliced
spring onions [finely sliced]
coriander (Chinese parsley) plants
leaves of mak khi hout (Kaffir lime) cut up finely
small chilli peppers, cut up and mixed with nam pa (fish sauce)
mint leaves
1 small bowlful of Chinese vermicelli, previously soaked in water and cut up

Method of Cooking

Put the pot, with 3 big ladlefuls of water, a pinch of salt, the coriander plants (with roots) and the mint, on the fire. When the water boils, put the pork bones in and continue boiling until what meat is on the bones comes off them. Take the pot off the fire and remove bones and meat. (Strain out also the coriander and mint.)

Replace the pot, now containing clear soup, on the fire. Add the small bowl of shallots and the slices of heuak kwai. When the shallots have become soft, add the small bowlful of Chinese vermicelli and continue until this too is cooked. Then add the slices of hard-boiled egg and [the flesh of] the fish. Mix well.

The soup is served in small bowls, with the [sliced] spring onion and the little bits of chilli pepper added to it. It may be eaten with a sauce made from shrimp paste and with assorted fried vegetables.

(Recipe No. 2 in the Cahiers of Phia Sing)

KENG SOM HOUA PA VA SAI HET SED

Soup made from the head of a Pa va and orange mushrooms

Of all the fish for which the Crown Prince fishes in the Mekong and its affluents near Luang Prabang, the Pa va (**Labeo dyocheilus**, page 43) is his favourite. We must suppose that the late chef at the Palace was regularly called on to cook this prized catch, and that the two recipes for Pa va which have survived in his Cahiers are the fruit of long and close experience. This one is for a soup and is linked, by the injunction that they be eaten together, with that for a salad of Pa va on page 158.

Ingredients

1 Pa va head, cut into quite big pieces, cleaned and left in a bowl
1 soupbowlful of het sed (a small orange mushroom), with the bottoms of the stalks cut off, and thoroughly washed
1 stalk of lemon grass, crushed and tied in a knot
3 thin spring onions (phak boua lai leung), washed and crushed
1 soupbowlful of no mai sum (preserved bamboo shoots, see page 154)
a pinch of salt
either padek or nam pa (fish sauce)
spring onions, chopped

Method of Cooking

Put about 1½ ladlefuls of water in a pot. Make sure it is a big ladle. Put the pot on the fire; add the pinch of salt, the lemon grass and the spring onions. Bring this to the boil, then put the fish head in. Bring back to the boil. Add either padek or nam pa, and the mushrooms. When the mushrooms are cooked, add the preserved bamboo shoots, to taste.

Take the pot off the fire and serve the soup in bowls with the chopped spring onion on top. The dish is to be eaten with Sa pa va. [The reference is presumably to Sa ton pa va, page 158.]

(Recipe No. 37 in the Cahiers of Phia Sing)

KENG SOM PA

The fish soup of Laos

It was Nang Ammone, a student of cookery in Vientiane, who originally showed me how to make this soup. Her version is the simple, classic one. I give it first, and then explain some interesting variations, including my own favourite.

Ingredients

½ kilo fresh fish (Pa kho, the snakehead (page 78) is best, but any respectable freshwater fish will do)
2 or 3 stalks citronella (lemon grass)
½ teaspoonful salt
½ teaspoonful MSG
2 soupspoonfuls nam pa (fish sauce)
1 large or 2 small tomatoes, quartered
3 spring onions, finely sliced into rondelles
2 soupspoonfuls Chinese parsley, chopped (French parsley may be used instead, although a Lao cook would never do this)
juice of half a lime

Method

Crush the citronella stalks. Put them, with the salt and the MSG, in a pot of water (say, three quarters of a litre) and set it to boil.

Clean, scale and wash your Pa kho and cut it into sections about 2 or 3 cm thick. When the water has boiled for 10 minutes, add the sections of fish and the nam pa. Let it come back to the boil; shortly afterwards add the tomato quarters. Keep it all boiling gently for 10 to 15 minutes, uncovered.

Take the soup off the fire. Remove and discard the citronella stalks. Add the sliced spring onions and chopped parsley.

Put a few drops of lime juice in each soup plate. Pour the soup in, making sure that each plate receives its share of fish, tomato, spring onion etc. Stir and eat.

Variations

1. In the south of Laos tamarind leaves or pulp are often added when the cooking is nearly finished, If you do this, do not put lime juice in the soup plates.

2. At Luang Prabang, and in the South too, chunks of pineapple core may be used instead of tomato quarters. This is very economical. The rest of the pineapple will serve as dessert. But the core has relatively little flavour; I recommend the modest extravagance of using some of the pineapple flesh in the soup. Another expedient, useful when tomatoes are not at their best and mangoes are in season, is to substitute pieces of green mango for the tomato.

3. Those who like fiery dishes will add to this soup whatever quantity suits them of fresh-ground chilli.

4. Some Lao cooks add to the water, along with the crushed citronella stalks, one or two 'fingers' of ginger and half a dozen slices of galingale root (both of which have previously been roasted in the oven or over charcoal). These are later discarded with the citronella, but they leave behind them a subtle flavour which does not at all overpower the soup but greatly enhances it. I warmly recommend this variation, worth executing with the ginger alone if galingale is not to hand.

5. I should also mention what might be termed the royal variation, since it comes from the Cahiers of Phia Sing. Recipe No. 11 therein is entitled Keng tom yum pa kho, and contains very simple instructions for making soup of the Pa kho. Into boiling salted water he puts thick sections of Pa kho, cut across the body, and a handful of uncooked rice. When the fish is cooked, nam pa and chopped lemon grass/garlic/shallots/Kaffir lime are added; and there is a final garnishing of chopped spring onion and chopped small chilli peppers, accompanied - "if you like it sour" - by some lime juice.

KHOUA GNU PA LEUM

Ingredients

1 piece of Pa leum (**Pangasius sanitwongsei**, page 65) about the size of a man's hand, deboned, washed and sliced into thin pieces, which are to be boiled in just enough water to cover, with a pinch of salt and some nam pa

3 dried chilli peppers, grilled ⎫
6 mak kheua waan (round, sweet eggplants), grilled and with the burnt skin removed ⎬ all chopped and pounded together to become the 'kheuang hom'
4 shallots, grilled
2 heads garlic, grilled ⎭

heads of 3 spring onions (the thin kind), chopped
leaves of 1 of the spring onions, finely chopped
1 sprig Chinese parsley, chopped
a pinch of salt ⎱ [already mentioned above, with the fish, but
nam pa (fish sauce) ⎰ more may be needed to correct the seasoning]
pork fat for frying
2 mak khi hout (Kaffir lime) leaves, finely chopped

Method of Cooking

Take out the boiled pieces of fish and pound them together with the 'kheuang hom' until they are well mixed. Add fish stock and mix well, until you have a thick paste. Taste this and make sure that it has the right saltiness.

Put the pork fat in the pan and put the pan on the fire. Fry the chopped spring onion heads until they turn brown. Take them out, leaving the fat in the pan.

Put the fish mixture in the pan to fry; stir it well. Taste and make sure that the mixture has the right saltiness.

Add the chopped Kaffir lime leaves and half of the fried spring onion heads, with the chopped spring onion leaves, to the mixture. Mix well. Serve it on a platter, sprinkling it with the remaining fried spring onion heads and the Chinese parsley. It is to be eaten with young cucumber and keng som (sour soup).

(Recipe No. 114 in the Cahiers of Phia Sing)

KNAP PA

Fish with pork

This, one of her favourite fish recipes, has been contributed by Princess Ouane Souvanna Phouma. She recommends making it with any scaleless fish, which in practice means choosing a catfish such as Pa ling, Pa khop, Pa sa ngoua, Pa khe, etc.

1 kilo fish (see above)
500 grams pork (which should not be too lean), minced
a piece of fried pork skin (kiep mu)
3 stalks citronella (lemon grass)
1 or 2 fresh chilli peppers
4 shallots
1 teaspoonful of salt
1 sprig of dill
4 or 5 spring onions
2 tablespoonfuls of fish sauce (nam pa)
banana leaf (or Alba paper)

Clean and debone the fish. Cut the flesh into bite-size pieces. (Or mince the flesh, if you prefer.)

Chop up the fried pork skin, the citronella, the peppers and the shallots. Combine them in a mortar with the minced pork, add the salt and pound the mixture.

Wash the dill and the spring onions, cut them finely and add them to the mixture with the fish sauce, mixing all well together.

Now you will need banana leaves for wrapping. (Alba paper is a possible substitute.) You can make 2 large or 6 smaller packages, as you prefer. (The thicker the package, the longer it takes to cook.) If you use banana leaves you will need 2 or 3 squares for each package. Lay the squares one on top of the other, so as to form an eight-pointed star, then deposit the fish mixture in the middle, fold the leaves tightly over the mixture and secure the package with a splinter of bamboo.

The packages are to be cooked on a charcoal fire, or under the grill. They will be ready, depending on their size, in 30 to 45 minutes.

KNAP PA (second version)

Stuffed Fish à la Laotienne

This ingenious recipe is the invention of Mrs Oudong Sananikone, who has succeeded admirably in taking a familiar Lao theme and developing it in a natural way, in cognisance of other cuisines. The quantities given are for 2 or 3 people.

1 Pa kheng (**Anabas testudineus**, page 74) of 250 grams
1 stalk of citronella (lemon grass)
3 shallots
5 cloves of garlic
½ bunch dill
2 leaves of mak khi hout (Kaffir lime)
1 egg, lightly beaten
breadcrumbs soaked in milk and squeezed
salt
MSG

Scale the fish, then cut it open along one side, from head to tail (being careful to leave both head and tail intact). Snip through the backbone at each end. Gut the fish and draw out also all the flesh and bones. Discard the bones and cut the flesh into small pieces. The skin of the fish must remain intact except for the cut along one side.

Chop and then pound in a mortar the citronella, shallots and garlic. Mix this with the pieces of fish. Add also the dill and mak khi hout, finely chopped.

Before stuffing this mixture back into the fish, Mrs Sananikone adds the beaten egg and the breadcrumbs in order to keep it moist; and salt and MSG. When the mixture has been inserted, the side of the fish may have to be sewn up. This will not be necessary if the fish is wrapped in aluminium foil, since the pressure of the foil will hold all together. But it is better to follow the traditional practice and wrap the stuffed fish in a piece of banana leaf, which contributes a certain flavour to the dish (lotus leaves are an alternative, and they too impart a special flavour).

The fish, sewn if need be and duly wrapped, is to be grilled over a charcoal fire or baked in the oven for 20 to 30 minutes.

To serve, open the packet and lay the fish, still hot, on a platter with sticky rice.

KNAP PA GNON

A Luang Prabang recipe for small catfish

Ingredients

5 pa gnon, **Pangasius siamensis**, page 61 - these are fairly small pangasid catfish - cut off their heads and tails, clean off all mucus, gut them, make diagonal cuts in the flesh (but not cutting right through), then salt them and leave them on a plate
3 stalks of citronella (lemon grass)
2 green chilli peppers
5 shallots
the above three ingredients are to be pounded together: when they are well mixed, add
2 pieces crisp fried pork skin
and this is then called 'the mixture'
minced pork fat, quantity equivalent to a hen egg
a pinch of salt
nam pa (fish sauce)
leaves of phak itu (basil)
some chopped spring onion

Method of Cooking

Mix the mixture in a large bowl with the minced pork fat; add the pinch of salt and fish sauce to taste. Then put in the fish and mix all well together. Put in the basil leaves and the chopped spring onion. Wrap all this up in a banana leaf packet, placing the fish alongside each other and fastening the packet on top with a sliver of bamboo, and put it on the grill to be cooked.

When it is cooked, serve the dish on a platter. It is recommended that the dish be eaten with Keng phak houm on (soup made with young leaves of **Amaranthus** spinach, a favourite vegetable of the Thai Dam tribes).

(Recipe No 44 in the Cahiers of Phia Sing)

KOY PA / KOY TIOUM
A fish salad with a difference

The staff of the Ecole Ménagère at Vientiane demonstrated to us every detail of this nourishing dish as it is taught by them.

½ kilo Pa pho (cleaned weight) (page 62) or other catfish
juice of 2 limes
2 mak kheua phoy (round green eggplants)
12 or more mak kheng (tiny pea-sized eggplants)
1 or 2 mak thua nyao (the very long green string beans)
4 or 5 spring onions
2 cloves garlic
1 fresh red pepper
2 rice cakes (khao khob - they are available ready-made in the market, having been prepared thus: cook sticky rice in the usual way, then form it in moulds into small cakes, dry these and subsequently deep fry them)
some mint leaves, and some Chinese parsley (optional)
and for the sauce
2 soupspoonfuls padek
trimmings of the Pa pho

Chop the flesh of the raw fish fairly fine and mix the lime juice thoroughly into it. (The effect produced by lime juice on raw fish is in some respects similar to that produced by cooking it.) Then squeeze the mixture to expel the juices, saving them for use later.

Prepare the other ingredients. The mak kheua phoy are cut into very thin rounds. The tiny mak kheng are left whole. The long green beans and the spring onion are cut into cross-sections. The cloves of garlic and the red pepper are chopped very fine. The rice cake is pounded to a powder. The mint leaves are left whole. As for the optional Chinese parsley, my advice is to embrace the option of omitting it; but if you use it, leave it whole too. All these ingredients are mixed with the fish on a platter.

At this stage you have made Koy pa. The dish is transformed into Koy tioum if you proceed to add a sauce, made as follows. Boil the padek and fish trimmings in 1½ cups of water, straining the result and adding to it the reserved fish-and-lime juice. The sauce may be served hot or cold.

To eat this salad, take a lettuce leaf, fold it over, stuff it with the fish mixture, fold it over again so that it forms a little packet, dunk this in the sauce and eat it.

KOY TIOUM (an alternative version from Nang magazine)

Nang magazine, which is celebrating its second anniversary at the beginning of 1975 and to which I extend my congratulations, regularly publishes recipes, of which the following specimen from issue No 1 of 1973 is characteristically clear and precise.

Ingredients (for 6 people)

1 kilo fish (cleaned weight), preferably Pa kheng (page 74), Pa va (page 43), Pa tiok (page 30) or Pa sa ngoua (page 56)
3 grams beansprouts or 30 grams mak thua nyao (very long green beans)
mak pi (banana 'flowers', preferably from the variety of banana known as koy thani)
10 shallots
10 large chilli peppers (mak phet nyai)
2 large slices of galingale (kha)
3 limes
½ soupbowlful nam padek
some khao khoua (uncooked rice, fried until golden and then pounded)
nam pa (fish sauce)
2 handfuls of various kinds of mint
salad leaves such as phak salat (lettuce) and phak i leut (**Piper** sp.)
forest leaves such as phak kat (**Brassica** sp.), phak kadone (**Careya sphaerica**), phak sa mek (**Eugenia zeylanica**) and phak hom pom (Chinese parsley), or phak hom thet (**Eryngium foetidum**, which has a Chinese parsley taste)

Method of Cooking and Eating

Chop the flesh of the fish into small pieces or slice it thinly. Add the juice of the limes and knead the fish to expel together, into a separate bowl, the fish juices and the lime juice.

Cut the banana 'flowers' very small and mix them with the fish. Add the beansprouts (or the mak thua nyao, cut up small), the khao khoua and the mint (chopped fine).

Put the nam padek in a pot on the fire and then add to it the reserved mixture of fish juices and lime juice.

Sear the shallots, chilli peppers and galingale on the fire, then pound them. Add the result to the pot of simmering nam padek, which now becomes the sauce (and may be allowed to cool).

Take a salad leaf and wrap in it some of the forest leaves and some of the fish mixture. Dunk the package in the sauce and eat it. (This recipe is godd for a picnic or family reunion.)

LAM I'EN

Eel baked in bamboo

The village of Ban Hom, which lies on the bank of the Mekong some 20 kilometres downstream from Vientiane, prospers in producing vegetables and tobacco (and marijuana) for the market of the capital city. The Lao will say of a girl who displays a strong will that "she is as strong as the tobacco of Ban Hom". However, the village could just as well be known for its bamboo, which grows there in great abundance and plays an important double part in this Ban Hom recipe, providing both the cooking utensil and an unique fragrance. (See the drawing opposite.)

2 swamp eels (I'en, page 89) of regular size, i.e. about 60 cm long
2 stalks of citronella (lemon grass)
1 head of garlic, i.e. about 8 cloves
3 shallots
1 soupspoonful chopped French parsley
½ cup phak itu (basil) leaves
6 pieces of galingale (about 2 millimetres thick)
2 soupspoonfuls nam pa (fish sauce)
1 teaspoonful MSG
a section of bamboo (see directions below)

Behead and gut the eels, and wash them very thoroughly to clear away the slime which coats their skins. Cut them into sections of about 2 to 3 cm.

Bat the citronella stalks with the flat of a heavy knife, then cut them in half. Peel and crush the cloves of garlic. Chop the shallots. Put all these ingredients, together with the chopped parsley and basil and the pieces of galingale, into a container with the nam pa and the MSG. Add the pieces of eel, mix everything up and let it sit for a while.

Meanwhile select a piece of bamboo about 8 to 10 centimetres in diameter. Cut it just below one joint and then just below the next joint. This gives you a container which is sealed at one end and open at the other. (By the way, it is good to choose young bamboo, which will give a better fragrance to the dish than older bamboo.)

Put the pieces of fish and all the other ingredients in which they have been 'marinating' into the bamboo and seal up the open end with strips. The bamboo and its contents are now baked over a charcoal fire, but not too close to it; the cooking must be slow. Allow 40 minutes. Then unseal the bamboo, which should be charred but not burned through, empty the contents on to a platter and serve hot with sticky rice.

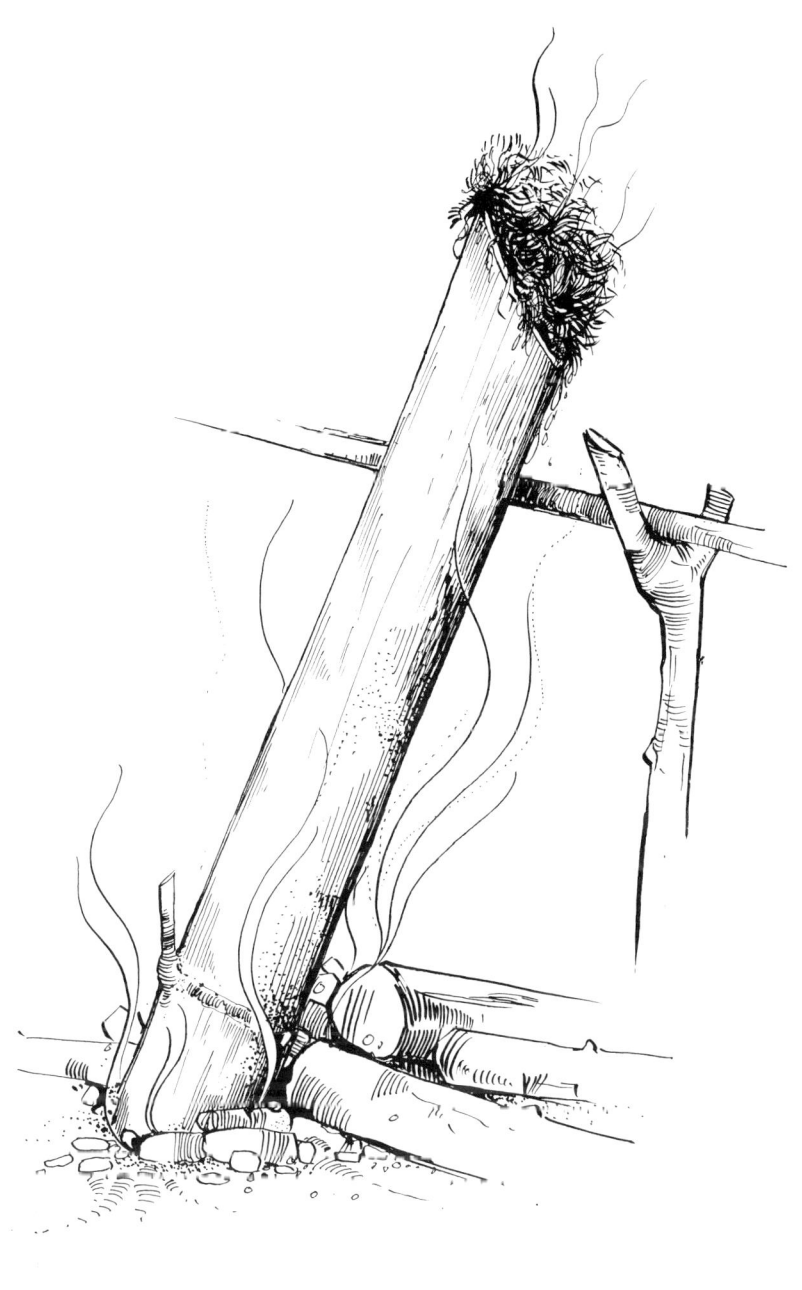

LAP PA

Fish tartare (or nearly so)

This is a popular dish in Laos. There is general agreement that it is best made with Pa tong (the featherback, pp 86, 87), but other fish with delicate white flesh may be used. Foreigners are likely to agree with me in preferring the Luang Prabang variation which is explained after the basic recipe.

1 kilo Pa tong
¼ cup sticky or other rice, uncooked
2 soupspoonfuls padek
4 or 5 large dried chilli peppers
3 fresh, small chilli peppers, thinly sliced
3 spring onions (including the green part), thinly sliced
1 slice galingale root, chopped very fine
a few mint leaves, if available
½ teaspoonful MSG
(and have nam pa, fish sauce, available in case it is needed)

Put the grains of rice in a frying pan and heat them, dry, until they are toasted. Then grind them as fine as possible in a blender or with pestle and mortar.

Remove the flesh from the fish (reserving the bones and other wholesome trimmings) and chop it very fine, until you have a smooth fish paste. Meanwhile add the fish bones and trimmings to about 1 litre of water and set it to boil gently for 15 minutes or so, to produce a fish stook.

Heat the padek in the bottom of a fairly large pot. Strain the fish stock and add it to the padek. Keep the whole hot.

Roast the dried peppers, then reduce them to a powder in a large mortar. Add the fish paste and pound some more. Next add the hot padek/fish stock mixture; this will have the effect of slightly cooking the fish. Add also the remaining ingredients and mix all well together with your pestle. Taste; add a little nam pa if the mixture is not salty enough.

The lap pa is then presented on a platter, accompanied by sticky rice and a separate bowl of vegetables. There should be plenty of vegetables. Cabbage, string beans, lettuce, radishes made into 'flowers', cucumbers carved according to one's fancy; all these are good.

The Luang Prabang variation - LAP MUONG LUANG

This will suit people who hesitate to eat fish which is raw or almost so. Moreover. it has a superior flavour. The directions come from Mrs Keut Thavonsouk.

The fish is roasted first. When the cooked flesh is chopped up and worked into a paste, the small bones are chopped with it. Having been softened by the cooking they will melt into the paste without much difficulty. But they are not the only addition. With the fish flesh are also chopped several each of: small round eggplants, shallots, cloves of garlic, all previously roasted and sliced to facilitate the chopping. Thus the fish paste which is produced has more body and flavour to it than in the basic recipe. Otherwise follow the basic recipe to the end. Then slice some shallots, fry them and strew them over the lap in its platter.

Another version - the LAP PA KHENG of Phia Sing

Recipe No 25 in the Cahiers of Phia Sing is devoted to explaining how an excellent Lap pa may be made from the Pa kheng (**Anabas testudineus,** page 74).

The directions require that the fish be scaled and that its head and gut be then removed together. The skin is to be cut at the tail and then 'rolled off' the body on a little stick, one strip at a time. The gut is to be emptied and cleaned, then placed with the eggs (if any) in a banana leaf package on the fire. The flesh of the fish is taken off the bone and chopped up. The skin is simmered with the head to make a fish soup, then removed and cut into slices. Thus does every part of the the fish contribute to the final result.

Sweet round aubergines are placed in charcoal ashes until they are blackened. 4 hot chilli peppers, 3 heads of garlic and 3 shallots are seared by the fire and then pounded with the aubergine and two slices of galingale, to form 'the mixture'.

The flesh of the fish and 'the mixture' are then combined. Some nam padek and some of the fish soup are added little by little during the process.

Finally, chopped Chinese parsley and chopped spring onion are added, together with the chopped skin, chopped gut, eggs (if any) and some chopped fried garlic over all.

LAP TIA (or LAP LEO)

A lap without lime juice

This is another recipe which was demonstrated to me at the Ecole Ménagère in Vientiane. The quantities given are variable. Well-off people would use plenty of fish and little or even no eggplant; poorer people the reverse. So the proportions which I give should not be taken too seriously.

Ingredients

1 fish (e.g. Pa tong, featherback, pages 86 and 87) of about 300 grams
4 round green eggplants ⎫
6 shallots ⎬ grilled and pounded together with a pinch
2 heads garlic ⎭ of salt
padek
100 grams fish liver ⎫ any large fish will do
100 grams fish intestine or stomach ⎭
2 or 3 tablespoonfuls of khao khoua (uncooked rice which has been fried until golden and then pounded)
several dried chilli peppers, grilled and pounded
a collection of leaves comprising phak hom po (mint); phak hom pom (Chinese parsley); phak pheo (**Polygonum odoratum**); spring onion leaves; and citronella (lemon grass) - all chopped except for the mint

Method of Preparation

Skin the fish and scrape the flesh off with a spoon, avoiding the bones. Pound the flesh with the pounded mixture of eggplant etc. Pound for a long time; the volume will increase as you go on.

Meanwhile you have boiled the padek in a pot of water for 5 minutes and strained it. This bouillon, which should be allowed to become lukewarm, is to be added little by little (as though you were making a mayonnaise) to the pounded fish mixture. You will find that you can work in a surprisingly large amount of the liquid while retaining the thick consistency of the mixture by diligent pounding.

After this, add the fish liver and fish intestine, both chopped into smallish pieces. Mix well, then add the khao khoua and mix again. Finally, add the prepared leaves. (The pounded chilli pepper is to kept apart.)

At this stage you have made your lap, unless you wish to follow a variation explained below and cook it.

Method of Eating

The Lap tia is to be served with a platter of vegetables which might consist of :
lettuce leaves
sliced cucumber
sections of rattan stalk (nuok vai) which have been grilled and peeled
young leaves of phak kat khao
dill (phak si)
leaves of phak ka dao (picked when the plant is in flower)
chopped green mango (in season)

Sticky rice is also served. The procedure is to take some sticky rice, knead it into a ball in the usual way and dip it into the fish mixture before eating it. The pounded chilli pepper is available in a saucer at the side for those who wish to add it. The vegetables are eaten at the same time.

Variations

In the South snails are often added to the lap - either little ones whole or (better) big ones minced. They must of course be cooked first and taken from their shells.

Another variation is to cook the lap after mixing it. The citronella and spring onion leaves would be added before the cooking, but the mint and Chinese parsley and phak pheo would be kept back and only put in when the cooking was complete. (About 10 minutes' cooking is enough.)

I have already explained that poorer people would use less or even no Pa tong and would increase the quantity of aubergines. They might also substitute Pa douk (page 58) for the relatively expensive featherback. The Pa douk would be gutted but their heads would be left on. After being grilled, they would be pounded, heads and all.

LON PADEK

One dish in which padek plays a principal instead of its usual supporting role.

This is the recipe of the Thavonsouk family, who are perfectionists so far as this dish is concerned. They stipulate the use of the rare and expensive padek of the Pa beuk; and it is this which gives the best results. However, other padek of good quality may be used instead. Note also that it is permissible to substitute for the pork an equivalent quantity of fresh catfish. Those who are in the grip of the western tradition that a dish should be either fish or meat, but not both, will wish to do this; and they will find that some Lao households do likewise. (The fresh catfish is not to be minced, as is the pork, but cut up into small pieces.)

Ingredients

8 to 10 pieces of padek of the Pa beuk (see above) weighing in all about 1/3 kilo
3 soupspoonfuls of the the liquid from the padek (nam padek)
½ kilo minced fresh pork (to include a little fat)
2 stalks citronella (lemon grass)
10 pieces galingale
10 leaves of mak khi hout (Kaffir lime)
5 cloves of garlic
10 spring onions
½ kilo shredded coconut
1 teaspoonful MSG

Method

Soak the pieces of padek in cold water, then wash them well. Remove any pieces of rice husk which may be sticking to them.

Crush the citronella stalks and cut them in half. Cut the lime leaves in half. Crush the garlic. Wash the spring onions, cut off their roots and chop them into pieces 2 to 3 centimetres long.

Add ½ cup water to the shredded coconut and squeeze to produce the first extraction of coconut cream. Them add 2 cups of water and squeeze again to produce the second extraction.

Heat the first extraction of coconut cream on a medium heat for about 20 minutes, until oil begins to form. Brown the crushed garlic in this, then add the minced pork and stir fry for 2 or 3 minutes. Next add the padek and the padek liquid and stir fry for 5 minutes. Now add the galingale, citronella, lime leaves, MSG and second extraction of coconut cream. Let it all boil gently for just over 25 minutes. Add the spring onions and continue cooking for 2 or 3 minutes more.

Serve with non-sticky rice. However, in many Lao homes it is the custom, when the juices in the dish have been eaten, to take some sticky rice and squeeze it together with such pieces of padek as are left.

This dish will keep for a long time, whether refrigerated or not.

LUK SIN PA

Steamed fish balls

These little fish balls can be bought ready made; but they are simple to prepare and have more than one use.

There is only one ingredient, as much fish meat as you need. (Almost any fish will do, but a good choice would be featherback, pages 86 and 87.)

The method is equally simple. Mince the fish meat, pound it to a paste, make small balls out of this and steam them for 15 minutes.

These fish balls may be used to good effect as an addition to soups, for example Keng phet (a piquant soup, popular in Thailand, featuring chilli peppers and coconut) or Keng cheud mu (a mild pork soup).

Alternatively they may be used as snacks or as something to be eaten at receptions. Spear them on toothpicks, dip them in boiling water to reheat them (if necessary) and offer them with a bowl of sweet and sour sauce, made from the following ingredients:

nam pa (fish sauce); lime juice; sugar; garlic and chilli peppers pounded together (optional); and a little ground roasted peanut for thickening

(Mrs Théothong Bounyarong)

MAM PA KOR

A recipe from Sithandone for pickling fish with khao khoua

Ingredients

6 soupbowlfuls of the flesh of Pa kor (**Gyrinocheilus aymoneri**, page 45 - no other fish will do)
1 soupbowlful of salt
cooked sticky rice (khao nyao souk), quantity equivalent to a hen egg
1 soupbowlful khao khoua (uncooked sticky rice fried until golden and pounded very thoroughly)
5 or 6 large pieces of galingale, cut up fine
½ soupbowlful of the intestines of the Pa kor, well washed

Method of Cooking

Cut the flesh of the Pa kor into small pieces and mix them well with the salt. Moisten the cooked sticky rice with water and mix that in too. Cut up the intestines and add them, mixing again.

Keep this mixture for two days, then add the khao khoua and the galingale and mix well once more. Put the result in an earthenware pot and keep it well sealed. It will be all right for several days. When the liquid rises in the pot, that it the sign that it is ready.

Mam pa kor is to be eaten with vegetables. Raw chopped chilli peppers and shallots are to be added to it.

MIENG PA

A way of presenting any whole grilled fish.

Four elements are presented together.

First, there is a large platter of raw vegetables and salad greens.

Secondly, Khao poun, the rice noodles which (with a different accompaniment) constitute the Laotian national dish.

Thirdly, you must clean suitable fish and grill them whole over charcoal.

Finally, a sauce is made with nam pa (or nam padek, i.e. the liquid part of padek), lime juice and scraps of hot chilli pepper.

Compose a mouthful from the first three elements, dip it in the sauce and eat it.

MOK KHAY PA

Steamed fish eggs

The Cahiers of Phia Sing contain two versions of this recipe, numbered 57 and 104. They are almost identical; but the former is slightly clearer, while the latter has a footnote which the other lacks. I present, therefore, recipe 54 with the addition of the footnote to 104.

Ingredients

1 soupbowlful of fish eggs, which have been stirred in water with a little salt so as to separate the eggs
1 piece of fish meat, deboned and minced, quantity equivalent to a duck egg
pork fat, minced, quantity equivalent to a hen egg
1 dried chilli pepper, seeded and soaked in water ⎫
5 shallots ⎬ chopped and pounded together
spring onions, chopped ⎭
some very small fresh chilli peppers
salt
nam pa (fish sauce)

Method of Cooking

Take the minced fish and the minced pork fat and mix them both together with the ground dried chilli pepper and shallots. When they are well mixed, combine them with the bowlful of fish eggs. Add salt and fish sauce to taste. Add also the spring onion and the small chillies, and mix well.

Take a piece of banana leaf, roll up the mixture in it and fasten the package with a 'bamboo string' [such as is used for tying packages in the market].

The package is then put in a steamer and steamed until it is cooked. When it is cooked, take the package out of the steamer, open it and serve the contents on a plate.

Footnote

This Mok khay pa usually needs the small chilli peppers and the pork fat; otherwise the fish eggs would set too hard. If you don't like them, take them out, but this is not the way to cook Mok khay pa.

MOK PA (Serves 4)

Savoury steamed fish

1 kilo (cleaned weight) of catfish, preferably Pa nang (page 57) or Pa kot (page 40)
3 stalks citronella (lemon grass)
3 shallots
1 head garlic
2 teaspoonfuls chopped galingale
1 teaspoonful salt
½ teaspoonful MSG
2 soupspoonfuls nam pa (fish sauce)
3 cups coconut cream
6 eggs, beaten
5 or 6 leaves of mak khi hout (Kaffir lime)
1 or 2 teaspoonfuls of chopped dill leaves

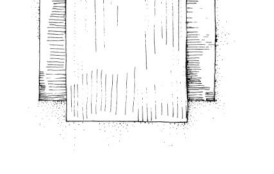

Clean the fish and cut the flesh into serving pieces or bite-size pieces, as you prefer.

Finely chop the lemon grass. Chop the shallots. Peel the cloves of garlic (you should have 6 to 8 from one head) and chop them too. Put these ingredients in a mortar with the chopped galingale and pound them.

Add the pounded mixture to the pieces of fish and season it all with the salt, MSG and nam pa. Then add the coconut cream and the beaten eggs. Mix all together.

Now you will need three rectangles of banana leaf. (If they are from a freshly cut leaf, hold them, each in turn and for a few seconds only, over a fire so as to soften them and to eliminate the risk that they will break during the cooking.) Lay these one on top of the other, as shown in the drawing, and then deposit the fish mixture in the middle, with fragments of lime leaf and a little chopped dill sprinkled on top. Fold the banana leaves up and over and secure them with a piece of split bamboo, as shown in the drawing on page 144.

Steam this package for half an hour. Then remove it from the steamer, undo it and transfer the contents to a serving dish. Mok pa is served with plenty of rice, which may be sticky or non-sticky.

In the south of Laos the beaten eggs would be omitted and the cooked mixture would therefore be less set and more liquid. However, the amount of coconut cream used would be much less.

MOK PADEK PHO KHA

Mok padek prepared in the fashion of merchants

Ingredients

3 pieces of padek, the meat only with all the rice husks cleaned off, cut into small bits and left on a plate
3 pieces of dried water-buffalo skin (grill them until they are cooked, then clean off the burned bits, cut them into strips about the size of a finger, wash them in water and leave them too on a plate)
2 heads of lemon grass (take only the soft bits and cut them into small pieces half an inch long)
5 heads of either the thin or the bulbous spring onion, sliced along their length [reserve the leaves for separate use later]
3 large chilli peppers, each cut into four
leaves of mak khi hout (Kaffir lime)
3 slices of galingale

Method of Cooking

When the above ingredients have been prepared, put them all in a pot and mix them well together. Add some water to keep the mixture moist. Then wrap it in a banana leaf package, gathering up the ends and fastening them on top with a splinter of bamboo. Grill it until it is cooked, then serve it on a platter; sprinkle some chopped spring onion leaves over it.

It is recommended that this dish be eaten with crisp fried pork skin and young cucumber.

(Recipe No. 46 in the Cahiers of Phia Sing)

MOK PA FA LAI

Stingray grilled in banana leaf

The species of stingray which inhabits the Mekong is described on page 90, and mention is made of the fact that it is especially well-known at the royal capital, Luang Prabang. It is not surprising that the personal recipe book of the royal chef should contain a recipe for it, as follows.

Ingredients

1 piece of stingray about the size of a man's hand, taken from the underside, cleaned of mucus and cut up into suitable small pieces
2 stalks lemon grass ⎱
2 very small green chilli peppers ⎬ chopped and ground together
5 shallots ⎰
spring onions, chopped (green part only)
10 leaves of mak khi hout (Kaffir lime)
a pinch of salt
nam pa (fish sauce)

Method of Cooking

Put the prepared pieces of fish into a big bowl, add the pounded mixture, mix well and add salt and fish sauce to taste. Add also the Kaffir lime leaves and some of the spring onion. Mix well together.

Use a banana leaf to wrap this whole mixture, in a crested shape [see drawing below] which you can fasten with a splinter of bamboo. Grill this until it is cooked.

Put the cooked mixture on to a plate and put the rest of the chopped spring onion on top.

(Recipe No. 48 in the Cahiers of Phia Sing)

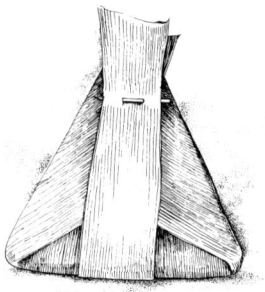

MOK PA FOK

A kind of steamed fish pâté

½ kilo Pa tong (featherback, pages 86, 87)
2 shallots
4 white peppercorns (or nearly 1 teaspoonful of prepared white pepper)
2 eggs, beaten
½ cup coconut cream
1 teaspoonful salt
½ teaspoonful MSG
2 teaspoonfuls nam pa (fish sauce)
2 or 3 small chilli peppers
some sprigs of dill

Scale your piece of Pa tong. Remove the flesh, discarding such bones as you can but ignoring the fine ones. Chop up the flesh and then pound it very fine.

Pound the shallots and the white peppercorns and combine them with the fish. Add the beaten eggs, the coconut cream, the salt and the MSG. Mix the whole well, so that it is of a smooth and creamy consistency and put it in little banana leaf baskets. Steam these for about 15 minutes. Or, if you wish, you may roast them on a charcoal fire.

Decorate the fish pâté (which is to be left in its banana leaf baskets) with thin rounds of chilli pepper (produced by slicing the peppers crosswise) and tiny feathers of dill leaf.

This recipe is the one used by Nang Lienne when she made the dish for us at the Ecole Ménagère in Vientiane. I have only one comment to add. It seems to me better to cut the rings of chilli pepper into smaller pieces, so that each mouthful of the fish pate will include a tiny piece of chilli. The contrast between the bland fish mixture and the hot chilli is agreeable.

Variations

(1) Add a little Chinese parsley root, well washed and chopped, to the shallot before pounding it.
(2) If making the dish with very small fish (Pa khao, for example) add a little rice flour, citronella, chilli (the dried kind, but soak it in water before using it) and garlic. These ingredients all go in to be pounded with the shallot.

NUNG PA

Steamed fish

2 kilos (uncleaned weight) fish (preferably Pa kot, page 70; but other kind of catfish for example Pa nang, page 57, will do)
½ kilo freshly grated coconut
6 leaves of mak khi hout (Kaffir lime)
½ cup phak itu (basil)
10 cloves of garlic, peeled and finely sliced
3 shallots, peeled and sliced
2 eggs
2 stalks citronella (lemon grass), cut very fine
1 cup spring onions, cut into pieces of 1½ cm
½ cup chopped French parsley
½ cup nam pa (fish sauce)
1 teaspoonful MSG

Clean the fish and cut it into sections of about 2 to 3 cm.

Mix the grated coconut with a cup of water. Squeeze it and set aside the resulting coconut milk.

Wash the leaves of mak khi hout and break each leaf into 5 pieces. Wash the phak itu. Save the leaves and discard the stalks. Pound the garlic and shallots in a mortar.

Break the eggs into a large container which can later be used for steaming. Beat them thoroughly; then add the fish and the remaining ingredients. Mix them well. Place the container, uncovered, in a steamer. Cover the steamer and cook for about 40 minutes. Serve while still hot.

This is one of the favourite recipes of the Thavonsouk family of Vientiane, given to me by Mr Thep Thavonsouk. I discussed with him whether the recipe could be adapted for use in an area where citronella, mak khi hout and phak itu are not available. He agrees that it would be feasible to use grated lemon peel instead of the citronella and to substitute for the other two ingredients some aromatic herbs such as marjoram and thyme. The result would be different, but recognisable as a legitimate variation on the Nung pa theme.

OR PA

A fish and vegetable stew

1 kilo (cleaned weight) of any fish of reasonable quality
300 - 400 grams of shredded coconut
2 stalks citronella (lemon grass), sliced very fine
3 shallots, chopped
6 cloves garlic, chopped
½ a dried chilli pepper, large size, previously soaked in water, chopped
2 teaspoonfuls of galingale, finely chopped
2 soupspoonfuls padek (more liquid than solid)
1 teaspoonful MSG
2 cups mak thua nyao (the very long string beans) cut into lengths of 2 cm
1 cup mak kheua phoy (small eggplants), each cut into 8 segments
2 soupspoonfuls spring onions, chopped
2 soupspoonfuls French parsley, chopped
6 leaves of mak khi hout (Kaffir lime), broken into small pieces

Cut the cleaned fish into serving pieces.

Add about half a cup of water to the shredded coconut and take the first extraction of cream. Set it aside. Then add 2 cups of water to the shredded coconut and take the second extraction. Reserve that also.

Pound the citronella, shallots, garlic chilli and galingale in a mortar.

Heat, over a moderate flame, the first extraction of coconut cream. After about 15 minutes the oil will begin to separate on its surface. At this point add the contents of the mortar and stir-fry for 3 to 4 minutes. Add the pieces of fish and stir-fry for another 3 to 4 minutes. Add the padek and MSG and stir-fry for another 3 to 4 minutes. Add the string beans and the eggplant and stir-fry for yet another 3 to 4 minutes.

Now add the second extraction coconut cream and let the whole mixture go on cooking for another 15 to 20 minutes until the vegetables are done. Add the remaining ingredients (spring onions, parsley and lime leaves). Leave the pot on the stove for just a few minutes more, then serve the dish hot with either sticky or non-sticky rice.

Variation

The dish can be made without using coconut cream. Simply substitute for the first extraction cream a soupspoonful or so of vegetable oil, and for the second extraction cream between ½ and 2 cups of water.

OR PA SA NGOUA

Ingredients

The head and tail of a Pa sa ngoua (**Kryptopterus bleekeri**, page 56), cut into pieces and washed
2 sweet young aubergines (mak kheua waan on), sliced lengthways and washed
1 handful white mushroom (het khao), to be washed after the bottoms of the stalks have been cut off
1 handful phak tam nin [a climbing plant, **Melothria heterophylla**, of which the chopped leaves are used]
1 stalk lemon grass
5 small chilli peppers
5 shallots
1 handful uncooked sticky rice, previously steeped in water for a while

to be put in a mortar and pounded together*

a pinch of salt
padek or nam pa (fish sauce)
spring onions, chopped

Method of Cooking

Put 1 big ladleful of water in a pot. Put the pot on the fire. Add some salt and the ground mixture. Bring all this to the boil. Then add the pieces of fish, the aubergines and the mushrooms. When the fish is cooked, add padek or nam pa, and the phak tam nin, to taste .

This is served in a big soupbowl, with the chopped spring onions sprinkled on top. It is to be eaten with young cucumber .

(Recipe No. 34 in the Cahiers of Phia Sing)

---

*The text says that only the last two of these ingredients are to be pounded together, but it seems clear that this is a slip and that all four are meant .

PA CHAO

A method of preserving fish used in the south of Laos

Ingredients

6 soupbowlfuls of fish, preferably Pa mak phang (**Hilsa kanagurta**, page 92) or Pa phone (**Cirrhinus microlepis**, page 33), but pieces of catfish such as Pa pho (page 62) or Pa hou mat (page 64) will do: if using the preferred fish, make deep cuts lengthwise in their bodies, down to the bone

4 or 5 soupbowlfuls of salt

1 kilo khao namak, which is sticky rice which has been cooked, allowed to cool, washed, and then mixed with 4 small discs, as sold in the market, of pheng lao which is a sort of lau-lau yeast, well pounded

Method of Preparation

Take the fish one at a time and put lots of salt into the cuts which you have made in their sides. Then leave them thus for 4 or 5 days, in a sealed jar.

Meanwhile prepare the khao namak, which is also to be left in a carefully sealed jar for 4 or 5 days to ensure the production of a suitably acid taste as alcohol is formed. (Only the solid in the jar will be used, not the liquid.)

On the 5th or 6th day, drain the khao kamak and mix it with the fish, one at a time as when you were salting them. Keep the result for one year, by which time the fish will have a good acid taste.

Method of Eating

Pa chao is eaten like Som pa, uncooked and accompanied by mak kheua (round aubergines). But it may also be sautéed with eggs. Either way, it is of course only the flesh of the fish, picked clear of bones etc, which is to be eaten.

PA KHEM

Salted fish in the manner of Xhieng Khouang

This recipe is a traditional way of preparing the small fish of the Province of Xhieng Khouang. The fish used may be Pa douk or other small catfish, or minnows such as Pa khao or Pa fède. (Pa khao is a fish of the genus **Rasbora**, page 22, and Pa fède is a related species.) These are preserved in the following manner, described to me by Nang Noi Nahaideo.

For each kilo of fish allow one small soup-bowlful of salt. Wash the fish well and let them dry off on one of those wide, shallow vanniers which are used for winnowing rice. Gut the fish and cut them up into pieces. Mix these thoroughly with the salt and store the mixture in a jar for 3 months or so. The jar should be full and the cover sealed with ash.

When the time comes to use the fish, there is a choice of two methods. One is to fry the pieces with chopped garlic and onion in oil. But the better and more traditional method involves a wider range of ingredients, including one which is a speciality of Xhieng Khouang and Sam Neua. There is a tree in those parts which produces a small fruit called mak maade. These little fruits are dried in the sun until they burst. The skins only are then grilled and pounded to a powder which has an agreeable and distinctive aroma and taste.

1 soupbowlful of the salted fish
1 or 2 young garlic plants
2 or 3 hot chilli peppers (of the larger size)
1 or 2 soupspoonfuls of fried and pounded sticky rice (khao khoua)
a little mak maade powder
mint, chopped

Sear the garlic heads (reserving the leaves) and the chillies, then pound the garlic heads and shred the chillies. Put them in a bowl; add the fish, rice, mak maade powder and chopped mint. Chop the garlic leaves finely and sprinkle them over the dish, which is now ready.

Variation - Salted fish in the manner of the South of Laos

In the South the small Pa soi (**Cirrhinus jullieni**, mentioned on page 33) is abundant in the dry season and is salted in the following manner. 5 soupbowlfuls of the fish, washed but whole, are well mixed with 4 soupbowlfuls of salt and then kept in a jar for 1 to 4 weeks, until the liquid begins to rise. At this time 4 or 5 sizeable pieces of galingale, cut up into small bits, are added, together with 2 soupbowlfuls of khao khoua (sticky rice fried until it is golden, but not pounded). The preparation is then complete, and the mixture will keep for a year or so.

PA PAN

Fried fish balls

Ingredients

250 grams fish meat, deboned
half a soupbowlful of grated coconut
7 chilli peppers
7 staks lemon grass
1 shallot
½ head garlic
} chopped and ground together

1 coffeespoonful nam pa (fish sauce)
3 coffeespoonfuls cassava flour (or other flour)
enough pork fat for frying the fish balls
3 spring onions, chopped

Method

Mince the fish meat thoroughly, then pound it into the ground mixture of chilli peppers etc. Add the grated coconut, the flour, the fish sauce and lastly the chopped spring onions. Mix well.

Make small balls (about the size of a pigeon's egg) from the mixture. Put the pan on the fire, put the pork fat in and, when it is hot, fry the fish balls in it until they are golden-brown.

The fish balls may be eaten with rice as a main dish (the quantities given being sufficient for 3 people). Or they may be eaten alone as a snack (what the Lao call khong wang - 'between meals').

(Mrs Théothong Bounyavong)

PA PHAO
Fish baked in clay

This is a countryside method of cooking fish, which can be used on picnics. All you really need is a fish and some suitable clay and a wood fire.

The best fish to use is a snakehead (pages 78 to 80). One weighing about 1½ to 2 kilos will do for four people. Do not behead or gut it. Simply wash it well.

The clay should be moist but not runny. Slurp it all over the fish, moulding it to the body until the entire fish is encased in a clay jacket about 1 cm thick. Leave no holes or gaps. If you have trouble with the tail, cut it off.

The wood or charcoal fire should be blazing merrily. Place the clay-clad fish upon it and leave it there for an hour. Then remove it and let it cool a little before breaking the clay and lifting this off. As it comes off it will reveal the white cooked meat; scales and skin will have stuck to the clay.

Eat the fish while it is hot. A suitable and simple accompaniment is tcheo (or tieo). This consists of 2 chilli peppers chopped small and put into a bowl with 2 teaspoonfuls of nam pa (fish sauce) mixed with 1 teaspoonful of fresh lime juice.

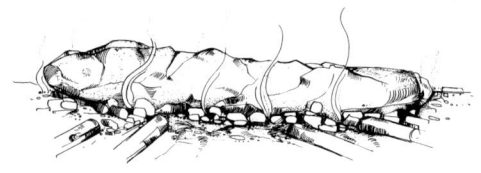

A more specific version of this recipe, from the South, has been given to me by Dr Khamlieng Pholsena, who recommends that the Pa kho (i.e. the snakehead catalogued on page 78) be invariably used, and that it should be alive when encased in its clay jacket. The weight of the clay will be sufficient to subdue the wriggling of smaller fish; large ones have to be stunned first. The clay used in the South is reddish; and 15 minutes on a lively fire may be enough to ensure the cooking. Dr Pholsena emphasises that the entire fish (except for the skin which is left adhering to the clay, and the bones) is to be eaten. He calls the dish PHAN PA KHO, in allusion to the method of eating it - in salad leaves, with phan khao poun (the Lao national dish, not everyone's idea of picnic fare but worth taking for this purpose).

PA SA NGOUA TCHUN NA SOM

Fried sheatfish with a sour sauce

Ingredients

6 pieces of Pa sa ngoua, cut to about the size of a finger (the thickness according to the size of the fish), washed in water, salted, fried until they become golden-brown and reserved on a platter
1 small tin of tomato paste
pork meat (to include a bit of fat), washed and finely minced, quantity equivalent to a duck egg
half an onion, cut into slices along its length
3 spring onions, the bulbs to be crushed and the leaves finely chopped
Chinese parsley, chopped
some small chilli peppers, chopped
a pinch of salt [may be needed to correct the seasoning]
nam pa (fish sauce)
pork fat for frying

Method of Cooking

Put a frying pan on the fire and put a spoonful of pork fat in it. When it is hot, put in the crushed spring onion. Then add the prepared pork meat and a little nam pa. When this is cooked, the fat having been absorbed, and of a golden colour, add the slices of onion and the whole contents of the tin of tomato paste and cook the mixture until it is fragrant. Add a bit of soup* to make it less sticky a paste. Taste for flavour. Then add the chopped spring onion leaves and some of the chopped chilli peppers. When they are well mixed in, take the pan down from the fire.

Arrange the prepared pieces of fish on a platter, then pour the mixture from the pan on top of them. Sprinkle the Chinese parsley and the rest of the chilli peppers over it, and serve.

(Recipe No. 103 in the Cahiers of Phia Sing)

[*The Lao almost always have a pot of soup at hand, to go with every meal, except perhaps breakfast.]

PA TEN

Jumping fish

Nang Noi Nahaideo, who comes from Xieng Khouang and who lived for many years in Sam Neua, has given me a detailed description of this characteristic dish of Xieng Khouang. In those northern parts of Laos there are no large rivers and most of the fish available are therefore small. This has its influence on fish cookery, which has to be directed not at large carp and catfish but at humble little minnows, harvested from the rice fields and streams, and the like.

½ kilo live minnows, either Pa khao or Pa fède (the former of the genus **Rasbora**, page 22, and the latter a related species)
150 grams of no mai sum (bamboo shoots which have been chopped up and stored dry for about a year, with rice and salt, in large earthenware storage jars)
2 or 3 stalks of citronella (lemon grass)
2 or 3 soupspoonfuls of nam padek (liquid from the padek jar - nam pa will do, but would not normally be available in the villages of the area)
1 handful mint, chopped
2 or 3 spring onions, chopped
2 or 3 young garlic plants, chopped (NB, not heads or cloves of garlic, but the foliage of the young plant)
a little powdered mak maade (see page 150)
a little MSG

Boil the preserved chopped bamboo shoots and the citronella stalks in something like 1 litre of water for 30 minutes or so, then strain it. Squeeze the no mai sum over the strained liquid in order to express all the juices. Then add the nam padek to the strained liquid; and put in also the mint, spring onions and garlic plants; and the mak maade and the MSG. This is the soup.

Wash the live minnows. Put them in one bowl, with the soup alongside in another. Take a spoonful of fish, dip it in the soup and put the combination into your mouth, when you will have the unusual sensation of the fish jumping about as you eat them. It is considered essential to take alcohol, normally lau-lau, with this dish.

PHAN KIEO PADEK

Ingredients

1 drinking-glassful* of nam padek, carefully strained
pork meat, minced, quantity equivalent to a duck egg
a piece of fish meat about four fingers wide (it and the pork meat are to be boiled in the nam padek, then removed, the fish deboned and the two pounded together)
4 stalks lemon grass, finely chopped
10 shallots, chopped ⎫ fried in pork fat until golden,
10 heads garlic, chopped ⎭ then pounded in a mortar
4 rice cakes (khao khob), ground
2 pieces of fried pork skin, cut into bite-sized pieces
1 portion of rice noodles (khao poun), cut lengthways into 3
2 sweet round aubergines, cut into bite-sized pieces
10 salad leaves
3 spring onions (the thin kind), chopped (heads and leaves)
2 sprigs Chinese parsley, chopped [and /or mint leaves]
10 young phak kadone leaves [these are forest leaves, **Careya sphaerica**]
1 small bowlful pork fat

Method of Cooking

Put the pork fat in a pot. Put the pot on a not very strong fire. Fry the chopped lemon grass in this, but do not let it turn brown. Take it out. Then pour out the fat from the pot. Put into the pot the nam padek, the chopped meat and fish, and the shallots and garlic mixture, all together. Stir; then add the fried lemon grass. Stir again. When this is well mixed add the ground rice cakes; mix well and make sure that they don't form lumps. Then add the chopped spring onions (heads and leaves). Stir and taste. Put on a platter and sprinkle the chopped Chinese parsley or mint leaves on top.

Take another platter. Arrange the salad leaves and the phak kadone leaves around the edge. Place the rice noodles in the middle, with the pieces of fried pork skin and of aubergine around them. To eat this, take a salad leaf, put bits of everything in it, wrap it up and put it in your mouth.

(Recipe No. 58 bis from the Cahiers of Phia Sing)

*about ¾ of an English measuring cup or almost an American measuring cup

PING PA

Barbecued fish

This is such a simple way of cooking fish that it is apt not to count as "a recipe". However, it is so good that it deserves this careful description, which I have had from Mrs Théothong Bounyavong, who directs the Domestic Science section of the Fa Ngum School at Vientiane.

Many fish are suitable for a barbecue. Among the best are Pa douk (page 58) and Pa seuam (page 54). Specimens weighing between 200 and 350 grams will be about the right size for cooking whole. (The technique may of course be adapted to deal with pieces of larger fish, such as the Pa eun, page 31.)

The fish is to be scaled (if it has scales) and gutted. Any barbels should be removed, but otherwise the head should be left intact.

Slanting incisions should be made in the sides of the fish (especially where it is thickest - the object is to help the heat to penetrate evenly into the interior of the fish) and the body of the fish salted all over.

There are two ways of gripping the fish. One is to take a pointed sliver of bamboo about 10 cm longer than the fish and to run it right though the fish, entering at the mouth and coming out at the tail. The other is to take a whole length of bamboo, split it from one end down to the last joint before the other end, open it out sufficiently to allow the fish (or piece of fish) to be placed inside lengthways, and then tie the split ends together to hold the fish firmly in place.

Whichever method is used, the fish can either be suspended horizontally over a charcoal or wood fire, or held over it at an angle of 45 or 60 degrees by sticking the bamboo into the ground close to the fire. The fish will have to be turned to ensure even cooking.

When the fish is cooked through, serve it with a green papaya salad, and som phak khak (pickled greens or pickled Chinese cabbage). This is a typical Lao way, but in the relaxed atmosphere of a picnic it is of course permissible to devise other accompaniments.

PONNE PA

An exotic purée of fish

½ kilo (cleaned weight) of fish, for example one of the catfish
1½ soupspoonfuls padek
¼ kilo mak kheua khao (round white eggplants)
3 dried chilli peppers, roasted and pounded to a powder
5 cloves garlic ⎫ roasted and roughly chopped
2 shallots   ⎭
1 spring onion, finely sliced
sprigs of dill
nam pa (fish sauce) to taste
garnishing of your choice

Bring the cleaned fish and padek to the boil in ¾ litre water and let it all simmer for 20 minutes. Take out the fish and debone it, leaving the stock to cool.

Meanwhile boil the eggplants for about 20 minutes, until they are tender. Then take them out and remove the outer skins.

Now pound the fish and eggplants and garlic and shallots together until they form a smooth paste. Transfer this to a mixing bowl; add some of the fish stock, the pounded chillies, the sliced spring onion and the chopped dill leaves, and mix it all together. If necessary, to achieve the right consistency (which should be that of a thick cream), add some more of the fish stock. Add also a little nam pa to taste.

The ponne pa is served on a platter, garnished as you please. The Lao liking for Chinese parsley need not impel you to use it, although they often do. I prefer to do a little cucumber-carving or to plant a few sprigs of dill, in Finnish fashion, on the surface.

What is important is that you should serve the ponne pa with a good variety of vegetables, which always accompany it to a Lao table, and with sticky rice.

SA TON PA VA

A comprehensive fish salad (flesh, skin, eggs and intestines)

The author envisages the capture of a female Pa va (**Labeo dyocheilus**, page 43), with eggs.

Ingredients

1 piece of Pa va 20 cm long by 12 cm deep (the thickness being whatever the thickness of the fish is), cut up into thin slices each 3 cm by 2 cm and dressed with salt and the juice of 5 limes

3 stalks of lemon grass, finely chopped
2 heads of garlic, sliced
5 shallots, sliced
2 dried chilli peppers, cut up } mixed together
1 piece of young galingale, cut up
3 leaves of mak khi hout (Kaffir lime) cut up finely

1 small bowlful of nam padek, cooked
the eggs of the Pa va (quantity equivalent to a hen egg), grilled in a piece of banana leaf
the intestines of the fish (sai pa), similarly treated [and cut up]
the skin of the fish (nang pa), boiled and then cut up
spring onions [sliced]
phak hom [mint leaves and Chinese parsley]
a pinch of salt [to correct the seasoning]

Method of Cooking

Take the slices of fish which have been marinated in lime juice, squeeze them to remove the liquid, then mix them with the kuang hom (i.e. the mixture of six ingredients referred to above). Add the nam padek (to your taste) and fish eggs, intestines and skin, all mixed together.

Taste the mixture. If it is not sour enough, take the lime juice [left over form the marinade and now containing some fish juices and blood], cook it and add it to the mixture to your taste.

Serve on a platter with the spring onion and mint leaves and Chinese parsley on top. The soup Keng som het sed [page 123] is to be eaten with this dish.

(Recipe No. 35 in the Cahiers of Phia Sing)

SOM KHAY PA EUN

The eggs of the large carp known in Laos as the Pa eun (page 31) are considered to be of excellent quality. Mrs Ngon Sananikone, whose reputation in the field of Lao cookery is unsurpassed, kindly explained how she prepares them.

2 complete ovaries from a Pa eun (weighing about 1 kilo each)
½ kilo (or more if you wish) of the meat of the Pa eun
sticky rice - enough to fill one American measuring cup when cooked
3 or 4 heads of garlic, i.e. about 25 to 35 cloves
salt
powdered bats' dung (kithia) (optional)

Pound the cloves of garlic in a mortar. Flake the (uncooked) meat of the Pa eun. Add salt, calculating the amount as follows; for each Chinese soup-bowl of meat, add that amount of salt which will fill the base of the soup-bowl when it is turned upside down. Mix meat, salt and garlic together, kneading it all with your hands into a sticky mass.

Meanwhile steam the sticky rice and wash it three times, so that the stickiness is diminished and the grains separate. Combine the rice with the salted fish mixture.

Now open the ovaries, slitting the protective membrane of each very carefully with a sharp, pointed knife. (The eggs inside are fragile, and you must try not to break them. Some will inevitably be broken, but the fewer the better.) Add salt (in the same proportion as explained above) to the eggs and incorporate them gently into the fish and rice mixture.

The result is to be placed in a bowl just large enough to contain it. Pieces of banana leaf are placed over the surface of the mixture and patted into place. A cloth is then tied over the top of the bowl to exclude the air as far as possible. Leave it thus for two nights (if you like the dish to be only moderately sour) or three (if you prefer it more sour).

Mrs Sananikone added that if a more compact pickle is desired one should add a pinch of Kithia, the powder used in the rockets which are fired over the Mekong at the Annual Rocket Festival at Vientiane. This sounded like an alarming, even explosive ingredient. I thought at first that it must be saltpetre, which is an ingredient of gunpowder and also has a use in preserving skins and meat. However, not so; I am told that it is bats' dung, which is used in the rockets and helps to increase their velocity. (Bats' dung is usually available in pagodas, which explains why the winning rockets are often those entered by the bonzes.) The dung is dried and powdered before being sold, whether for rocketry or pickling

SOM PA

Pickled fish

The Lao like pickled fish, and the business of pickling it is taken seriously. One expert is Nang Phao, who sells her particularly delicious product at the Talat Khok Pho evening market just outside Vientiane. The directions which follow are those which she gives - with, I hope, some of her salty style still evident in translation.

Fish from the carp family are regarded as the best subjects for pickling. Nang Phao recommends Pa khoui lam (**Labiobarbus lineatus**, page 41) but says that other kindred fish will do instead, so long as they are of a suitable length (15 to 20 cm).

2 kilos Pa khoui lam or similar fish
2 to 4 litres (the more the better) of nam muak, which is water which has been used for soaking and washing rice
salt - 'less than the size of 2 eggs'
4 whole heads of garlic
2 teaspoonfuls MSG
cooked sticky rice - 'about the size of 4 eggs'
a piece of banana leaf about 25 cm across

Scale and gut the fish (leaving the heads in place). Wash them well in ordinary water, making sure that all traces of blood and of the innards are washed off. Make a shallow cut along each side of each fish.

Using the flat of a heavy knife, crush the bodies and heads of the fish gently. Wash them again in ordinary water, and then for a third time in nam muak. Shake off all excess water. Put the fish in a large recipient.

Crush (without peeling) all the cloves of garlic from your two heads. Wash the sticky rice in nam muak and leave it in a separate bowl.

Now the action begins. Add the salt to the fish and start to squeeze them gently. (Note that from now the squeezing process should last for between 30 and 60 minutes.) Add the garlic and MSG and - squeeze! The squeezing should be gentle and should be applied all over the bodies of the fish.

Next add the sticky rice and go on squeezing until your hands are tired - 'then you'll know that the salt, garlic and sticky rice have got into the bodies of the fish'. Taste it with the tip of your tongue and see whether the taste is saltier than the taste of your own sweat, as it should be. ('If so, the pickled fish will taste just right when it's done. You can get rid of what you tasted by spitting . . . ')

You finish squeezing, then finally put the fish in a bowl (a rectangular plastic bowl, barely longer than the fish themselves, would do well), packing them tightly in layers and lining them up nicely one on top of the other. Then push them down gently so that they stick together. Use the piece of banana leaf to cover the fish in the bowl, trimming it for an exact fit and pressing it down on to the fish to make as near air-tight a cover as you can. Take a stone, about the size of the palm of your hand and well washed, and place it on top. 'Some folk add a little nam muak after they put the stone on top but this is not necessary.' Do not peep in or lift the banana leaf while the pickling is in progress - if air gets in, the pickled fish will not smell good. Leave it all in a cool place (80° to 90°) for 2 or 3 days.

After this time a white liquid will appear on top of the fish, and will seep up through any cracks in the banana leaf or round the edges. This means that the fish are ready to serve.

Eat the pickled fish as they are, with sticky rice. Or fry them first with chopped shallots, and some fresh red chilli pepper if you wish, and then eat them with sticky rice.

Note that this method of pickling is intended to give the fish a good taste rather than to preserve them. The pickled fish will only be good for a few days.

SOUSI PA   (Fish with coconut cream)

This is the best-known of the Lao fish dishes which require coconut milk. The recipe given below is an expanded version of that given in the Lao cookery book cited in the bibliography under Lao Womens' Association.

½ kilo (cleaned weight) of good quality catfish or snakehead
3 or 4 large dried chilli peppers
2 small heads garlic (i.e. a dozen or more cloves)
3 leaves of mak khi hout (the Kaffir lime)
1 slice galingale
2 heads citronella (lemon grass)
1 cup thick coconut cream (first extraction)
3 cups thin coconut cream (second extraction)
a little nam pa (fish sauce)
½ teaspoonful salt and ½ teaspoonful MSG
2 tablespoonfuls chopped peanuts (optional)
a few sprigs of boua la pha (**Ocimum gratissimum**, a sort of basil)
4 or 5 small dried chilli peppers, pan-fried

Cut the fish into serving pieces.

Roast the large dried peppers, then pound them to a powder. Finely slice the cloves of garlic. Chop up the lime leaves and the galingale. Slice the lemon grass as finely as possible. Add all these ingredients to the pounded pepper in the mortar and pound until you have a smooth paste.

Heat the thick coconut cream in a saucepan, over a low to medium flame, until (after about 15 minutes) the oil becomes visible on top of it. At this point add to it the spicy paste which you have already prepared and stir it all well, so that a fine smell comes up from the mixture. Then add the fish, followed by a little nam pa, and stir some more. Next add the second-extraction coconut cream, with the salt and MSG, and continue cooking until the fish is ready. (The cooking time will depend on the thickness of the pieces of fish, but should not be more than about 20 minutes. Shortly before the cooking is finished the chopped peanuts may be added.)

The sprigs of basil and fried dried chillis are used to garnish the dish.

Another version - the SOUSI PA GNON of Phia Sing.

Having been told that this is the favourite dish of His Majesty The King, I have made space to include a summary version of the Palace recipe for it (Recipe No. 10 in the Cahiers of Phia Sing).

6 of the small Pa gnon (**Pangasius siamensis**, page 61) are needed. Cut off heads and tails, gut them, wipe all mucus off the bodies, salt them

and leave them aside. Take the first and second extractions of coconut cream from one coconut. Pound together 2 large dried chilli peppers (previously soaked in water) and 7 shallots.

Set the first extraction of coconut cream to boil and wait until it becomes creamy. Them add the pounded mixture and stir until a good smell is given off. This is the signal to add the prepared fish, one at a time and stirring well so that the whole of each fish is thoroughly exposed to the liquid mixture. This done, add enough of the second extraction of coconut cream to cover the fish. Cook for about 15 minutes. Correct the flavour with salt and nam pa if need be; and add chopped Kaffir lime leaves at the end of the cooking. The dish is served with chopped spring onion sprinkled on top; also chopped Chinese parsley and chopped small chilli peppers.

TCHUN PA   (Fried fish à la laotienne)   (Serves 4)

1 Pa kho (snakehead, page 48) weighing about 1½ kilo (uncleaned)
2 teaspoonfuls salt and 1 teaspoonful pepper
300 - 400 grams tomatoes (preferably cherry tomatoes), quartered
4 cloves garlic, peeled and chopped very fine
1 soupspoonful flour in ½ cup water
¼ litre (1 cup) vegetable oil for frying
½ cup spring onions, chopped into sections 2 to 3 cm long
1 soupspoonful sugar
1 soupspoonful nam pa (fish sauce)
1 teaspoonful MSG

Clean the fish and score it diagonally on both sides. The cuts should be made fairly close together (say, 1 cm apart) and should go right down to the bone. Leave the head in place because there is good flesh in the cheeks. Season the fish.

Heat the oil in a wok large enough for your fish. Fry it until the skin of the fish turns brown and crisp. (Since only part of the fish will be in the oil at any given time you will have to spoon hot oil over the other parts and turn it over at least once in order to ensure that it is all cooked. The shape of the wok is such that you can shift the fish around in it quite easily.) Remove the fish, pour out what oil is left and clean the wok.

Put the wok back on the fire with 1 soupspoonful only of oil. When this is hot, brown the chopped garlic in it. Add the tomatoes, spring onions, sugar, nam pa and MSG. When this is all cooked, stir the flour in its ½ cup of water and pour that in too. Continue to cook, stirring, for another 3 minutes. Then pour the mixture over the fish and dish up.

TIEO PA KA TAO

A speciality of the south of Laos, made from small sun-dried fish

Ingredients

30 Pa ka tao (This term requires explanation. It is used of a mixture of small fish such as Pa tep and Pa sieu, catalogued on pages 20 and 23. These have been salted and sun-dried, then stuffed into a large section of hollow bamboo, which may be even 1 or 2 metres long, sealed with earth and kept for up to a year.)
1 piece of fresh fish, of any kind
10 shallots
3 or 4 mak phet nyai (large chilli peppers) or more if you like the dish to be very hot
2 or 3 pinches of salt
2 soupspoonfuls nam padek

Method of Cooking

Take the 30 Pa ka tao out of their bamboo container and grill them until they turn golden-brown; this will only take a minute. Take off their heads and gut them. Then pound them thoroughly with the salt.

Sear the shallots and chilli peppers in hot ashes until they are done, then skin them and pound them into the fish mixture.

Grill the piece of fresh fish or cook it in the nam padek. Bone it and add the flesh to the existing fish mixture. Add a little nam padek. Taste, and add more if necessary.

Note. Some people like it to have an acid taste, so add a few drops of lime juice. Or, in the mango season, they may chop up finely some green mango and add this to the mixture.

Method of Eating

Tieo pa ka tao is eaten with uncooked mak kheua (the round aubergine) or cucumber, together with green vegetables (cabbage, phak kat etc) cooked in water.

(Miss Naly Abhay)

TOM KHEM PA   (a sweet and salty fish dish)

1 snakehead (Pa kho, page 78) of 1½ to 2 kilos (uncleaned weight)
1 head garlic, i.e. about 8 cloves
3 shallots
2 stalks citronella (lemon grass)
10 pieces galingale
10 pieces ginger
5 soupspoonfuls sugar
2 soupspoonfuls vegetable oil
3 soupspoonfuls nam pa (fish sauce)
1 soupspoonful soy sauce
1 teaspoonful MSG
4 duck eggs, hard-boiled

Cut off the head and tail of the snakehead (saving the head for soup), gut it and scale it. Then cut the fish across into slices 1½ centimetres thick.

Crush the cloves of garlic (without peeling them first). Crush and chop the citronella. Chop the shallots. Chop the pieces of galingale and ginger.

Put a wok on the fire. As it becomes hot pour in the sugar, which will melt and turn brown. Take care that it does not burn. Add the vegetable oil and fry in this mixture the garlic, shallots, citronella, galingale and ginger. Next add the pieces of fish and stir-fry for a good 3 minutes. This done, add the nam pa, soy sauce and MSG and stir-fry for 5 minutes more.

Now add 3 cups of water and the hard-boiled eggs and let the whole mixture boil gently for 30 to 40 minutes until the liquid is reduced to less than half of what it was. The eggs will turn brown, and this is another sign that the dish is ready. Serve with non-sticky rice.

TOM SOM PA PHA ONG   (a kind of Lao turtle soup)

Buy a Pa pha ong (page 96), remove its flesh and cut it into large or small pieces, as you wish. Boil for 15 minutes or so in plenty of water some crushed citronella stalks with grilled heads of garlic, onions, ginger and galingale. Then add the pieces of turtle and continue simmering for 30 minutes (or 45 minutes or even more if you have bought an elderly turtle). Almost at the end of the cooking add some tamarind leaves; and at the last moment some finely chopped spring onion.

TOM TCHEO

A fishy dressing for rice

Tom tchéo is for rice what Bolognese sauce is for spaghetti. That is to say, it is more than a sauce or dressing, yet is not intended to be eaten by itself. Any fish will do for this recipe, but you will save yourself some trouble if you choose one, for example a catfish, which is free of small bones.

1½ kilos (uncleaned weight) fish
2 soupspoonfuls padek (more solid than liquid)
3 shallots
1 head garlic
2 fresh chilli peppers, small size
1 teaspoonful MSG
2 teaspoonfuls Chinese parsley, chopped

Gut and clean the fish. If necessary, in order to fit it into your cooking pot, cut it up; but do not discard any of it. Bring 2 cups of water to the boil in the pot. Add the fish and bring the water back to the boil. Then introduce the padek, which is not put directly into the pot, but into a sort of bamboo basket (of which a drawing appears overleaf), called a Ka sot or Ka sor. Hold it over the cooking pot and spoon into it the 2 soupspoonfuls of padek. Then lower the basket into the pot, where it should stay for 5 minutes only while the water boils gently. Remove it when the 5 minutes have elapsed and discard the contents.

While the fish goes on gently boiling (which it is to do for another 20 to 25 minutes), roast the shallots and the chilli peppers and the whole head of garlic in the oven or over a charcoal fire or in hot ashes. (Wash them afterwards if you use hot ashes.) Then pound them together in the mortar just as they are (there is no need to peel them) and put them aside.

When the fish is cooked, lift it out into a bowl. Remove bones, skin, fins and head (having first extracted any meat from the head) so that there is nothing left in the bowl but the meat. Mash this up. Pour over it most of the liquid from the cooking pot, straining it as you do so in order to keep out rice husks which may have escaped from the padek basket. (Do not pour in the last dregs from the cooking pot.) Add the contents of the mortar and mix them up with the mashed fish and the liquid. Then add the MSG and the Chinese parsley (almost compulsory on this occasion, but not quite, thank goodness).

The Tom tchéo is served with rice, either sticky or non-sticky. Rice is put on the plate first and the Tom tchéo spooned over it.

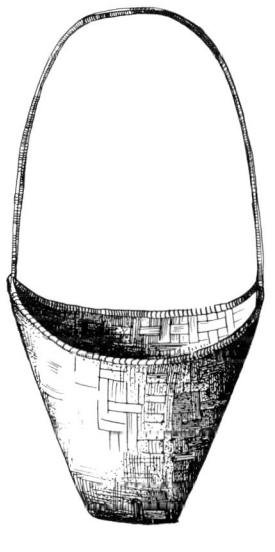

RECIPES FROM NEIGHBOURING COUNTRIES

So that the reader may compare Lao fish recipes with those of neighbouring countries in South East Asia I have added this little section, which provides a sampling of recipes from Burma, Thailand, Cambodia and Vietnam.

Had I more knowledge and a greater gift for synthetic survey, I should attempt to relate these regional recipes to the cuisines of India and to those of China. As it is, I must be content to observe that there are, of course, connections and that a historical and cultural study of them would be of great interest.

BURMA

Although Burma is rich in seafood, something like 80% of the fish consumed by the Burmese are freshwater fish. This is what the people strongly prefer. Many of them apparently find that eating sea fish makes them feel drowsy! Whether or not their preference is well-founded, it must be said that they have excellent freshwater fish and interesting ways of preparing them. One such is Mohinga, the national dish of Burma.

Many of the fish dishes of South East Asia arouse more interest than appetite on the part of Western visitors. "Interesting," we exclaim, declining a second helping. Mohinga does not fall into this category. It is delicious and its appeal seems to be just as strong to foreigners as to the Burmese.

All dishes which are both complex and popular exist in many different versions. So it is with Mohinga. The version presented here is essentially that of Naw Bway Htoo, whose Mohinga was the first I ever tasted; but it is only one among many.

MOHINGA

800 grams (½ viss) Nga gvi (**Heteropneustes fossilis**, a catfish)
2 stalks lemon grass, crushed
200 grams fish sauce (ngan-pya-ye)
2 or 3 chilli peppers (preferably fresh, but dried will do)
½ teaspoonful turmeric powder
    400 grams onions, finely sliced
    cooking oil
    4 cloves garlic   ⎫
    1 small piece fresh ginger   ⎬ pounded together
    ½ stalk lemon grass   ⎪
    2 more chilli peppers   ⎭
coconut cream (the product of half a coconut)
70 grams (4 ticals) rice flour   ⎱ roasted light brown in a
50 grams (3 ticals) dhal powder ⎰ hot dry pan before use
a 20 cm section of banana trunk, cut from high up
400 grams onions
3 duck (or 4 hen) eggs, hard-boiled
2 kilos rice noodles, previously cooked
    lime wedges
    more pounded chilli pepper (perhaps in oil)
    fried cloves of garlic
    fried onion rings
    Burmese bean patties (bajos)

Clean the fish, but leave the head in place. Set it to boil in just enough water to cover, with the remainder of the first batch of ingredients. Do not let it cook for long; 5 minutes should do. Then take the fish out and remove the flesh from it in little bits.

Turning to the second column of ingredients, fry the sliced onions golden brown. Add the pounded mixture of garlic etc. When a good aroma arises, add the flesh of the fish. Remove from the fire and keep aside.

Mix the coconut cream with the reserved fish broth and nearly 2 litres of water. Bring this to the boil. Meanwhile mix the rice flour with a little water; and do the same with the dhal powder. Add both to the main brew, stirring the while. Peel the section of banana trunk and slice it thinly. Cut the remaining onions in quarters. Add these ingredients. When they are tender, add the fish mixture, a pinch of salt and the eggs.

Now you have your hinga. It remains to place the mo, or rice noodles, in bowls, one for each person. Then ladle the hinga over it. Each guest should add what he wants from the accompaniments listed in the fourth column of ingredients. The Burmese bean patties are especially good.

RECIPES FROM THAILAND

KENG PHET PLA DOUK (Catfish curry)

Keng means, roughly, soup and phet means hot. There is a wide range of Thai dishes of this kind. This one, for catfish, has its counterpart in Laos, which may well be derived from Thailand. The recipe is that of Mrs Swate Komalabhuti.

Ingredients
1 kilo of Pla douk (pages 58 and 59): behead and clean the fish, slice the meat off the backbone and cut it into small pieces
5 cups coconut cream (first and second extractions)
1 cup curry paste (see below)
makrut (Kaffir lime) leaves, torn into small pieces
krachai (**Kaemferia pandurata**) roots, cut in long thin strips
nam pla (fish sauce)
fresh hot chilli peppers, seeded
horapa (sweet basil) leaves, without stems
and for the curry paste
7 large dried chilli peppers, seeded and previously soaked in water
1 teaspoonful salt
1 teaspoonful black pepper
2 teaspoonfuls caraway seeds
1 teaspoonful coriander root
2 teaspoonfuls coriander seeds
1 teaspoonful finely shredded makrut (Kaffir lime) rind
2 teaspoonfuls finely shredded citronella (lemon grass)
1 teaspoonful finely shredded galingale
1 tablespoonful chopped shallots
2 tablespoonfuls chopped garlic
1 teaspoonful kapi (shrimp paste)

Method of Preparation
The curry paste is made as follows. Pound the chilli peppers with the salt. Add the other ingredients, pounding as you go. Pound very fine; the finer the paste the better the curry.
Bring the coconut cream to the boil and keep it simmering until the oil separates. Then add the curry paste, the makrut leaves and the tiny eggplants. Keep all gently boiling until it thickens, then add the fish, with fish sauce to taste, and continue cooking for another 15 minutes. Add the chilli peppers and basil leaves, stir well and serve.

HO MOK PLA LAI

(Steamed eel with coconut milk and curry paste)

Ingredients
2 swamp eels (**Fluta alba**, page 89)
2 tablespoonfuls nam pla (fish sauce)
½ kilo grated coconut, to provide first and second extractions of coconut cream
leaves of **Morinda citrifolia** (Thai yo, Lao nho ban) or one of the various cabbage leaves
spring onion, chopped
leaves of makrut (Kaffir lime), torn into small bits
and for the curry paste
2 large dried chilli peppers, previously soaked in water
2 tablespoonfuls citronella (lemon grass), shredded
1 tablespoonful shallot, chopped
1 tablespoonful garlic, chopped
½ teaspoonful grated rind of the fruit of the Kaffir lime
1 teaspoonful finely sliced galingale
1 tablespoonful salt
6 peppercorns

Method of Preparation
Make the curry paste by pounding together the ingredients listed (without worrying too much about the quantities - those given are for general guidance rather than scrupulous observance) and adding enough coconut cream (first extraction) to make a thick paste.

Clean the eels of slime and dress them in sections free of skin and bone. Put the fish sauce in a bowl, add the pieces of eel and stir them around. Then add the curry paste and mix well.

Prepare banana leaf packages. Place a yo or cabbage leaf in the middle of each, put some of the fish mixture on the leaf and pour some of the remaining (second extraction) coconut cream over it. Sprinkle the chopped spring onion and shredded Kaffir lime leaves on top of each such confection, close the packages with toothpicks or slivers of bamboo and steam them for half an hour.

Variations
The recipe may be used for other fish, in the same way as the Lao equivalent, Mok pa.

Some cooks add a raw egg to the curry paste, when mixing the pounded ingredients with the coconut cream.

The ingredients of the curry paste may be varied. Grated coriander root is one possible addition.

PLA PRIOWAN   (Fried fish with ginger sauce)

This dish may be prepared by frying whole fish (e.g. **Kryptopterus** sp., Pla neua on in Thailand, see pages 55 to 57) or by frying slices of a larger fish such as **Ophicephalus striatus** (Pla chon in Thailand, see page 78).

The fish is to be cleaned and dried. If using whole fish, make slanting cuts in each side, down to the bone, to form a diamond pattern. Make a batter from 1 teaspoonful of salt, 1 cup of cassava (cornflour), 1 tablespoonful of oil and ½ cup of water. Dip the fish in this and fry them until brown. Drain.

Meanwhile the ginger sauce has been prepared thus. Soak 9 dried fragrant mushrooms in water for a few minutes, then drain them and chop them very fine. Put them in a pan with 4 tablespoonfuls of vinegar, 2 tablespoonfuls of chopped spring onion leaves, 1 tablespoonful of soy sauce, and 4 tablespoonfuls each of sugar and of red pickled ginger (chopped). Boil all this for 5 minutes, then add a tablespoonful of cassava, blended with a little water, and continue stirring until it is cooked (about 15 minutes more).

The ginger sauce is poured over the fish, which is garnished with parsley (and chilli peppers if you wish).

PLAHENGPAD   (A Thai way of frying dried fish)

This is a recipe for dried snakehead (**Ophicephalus micropeltes**, Pla chado in Thailand, page 79).

The fish is to be roasted over a slow fire. Turn it from time to time. When it is done, beat it with a pestle to loosen the skin, then remove the skin and bones and pound the flesh well, so that it is free of lumps.

Cut some pork fat into thin strips and heat them in a pan over the same slow fire. When they are crisp, drain them and keep them aside. Use the hot lard in the pan to fry some chopped shallots until they are brown and crisp. Drain them also.

Next, fry the pounded fish in the same hot lard, stirring well. When it is done, sprinkle a little sugar over it and add the crisp pieces of pork fat. Stir, then add the fried shallots on top. The skin of the fish may also be fried crisp, in pieces, and used as additional garnishing. The dish should in any case be accompanied by pieces of water melon or pineapple.

FIVE CAMBODIAN FISH RECIPES

The traditional cuisine of Cambodia has been described as the most arduous in the world for the cook and the most pleasing to the eye of the diner. The following recipes, of which the first three come from an admirable monograph by Professor Hellei, may not quite warrant either superlative, but are full of interest.

SAMLA MCHOU BANLE (acidulated fish soup)

This, the most popular soup in Cambodia, is a combination of fish and vegetables with an acid flavour.

Miscellaneous little river fish and freshwater shrimp, duly cleaned, constitute the first element.

The vegetables may include Tralach (gourd or vegetable marrow), Trap ropou (round aubergines, see page 109), Peng pas (tomatoes), Trakuon (water bindweed), Pralit (water lily) and Kra ao chhouk (lotus buds); each fitly prepared.

The third element consists of condiments which are chopped and then pounded in a mortar with a little garlic. These should include tamarind, citronella, galingale and leaves of Ma am (**Limnophila confreta**).

Fourthly comes Prahok (a fermented fish product, akin to Padek, page 104) which is pounded to a paste and added to boiling water with salt and some Tuk trey (fish sauce). The fish are then put in, followed by the vegetables and condiments and the whole cooked for 20 minutes, when it is ready to serve.

KHOR TREY (a more exotic fish soup)

The basis of this soup is a sauce made by heating palm sugar until it is caramelised and then adding Tuk trey (fish sauce).

The fish may be snakehead again, or Trey pruol (**Cirrhinus auratus**, page 33) or **Trey sanday** (**Wallago attu**, page 52) or the small Trey linh (**Thynnichthys thynnoides**, page 40). In the last case the fish are left whole after being gutted; the others would be cleaned and cut into convenient pieces. The fish or pieces of fish are left to stand for an hour or two in a bowl with salt, dark soya sauce, pepper and crushed garlic. Then, the caramelised sauce being ready in a large pan, the fish are added. When the sauce has been boiling for ten minutes, with the fish in it, cold water is added. The fire is kept high and more cold water added whenever necessary, but never very much at a time, until the fish is well cooked. (If Trey linh has been chosen, the cooking will go on for 10 hours or more, with a little vinegar or rice alcohol added, so that the fish and their bones dissolve completely.)

TREY AING (grilled fish in the Cambodian style)

This is a common accompaniment for rice. As Professor Hellei remarks: "Le petit peuple se sert de petits poissons vulgaires simplement grillés à la braise avec de la saumure ou des légumes conservées". But he goes on to give a summary account of how the dish is prepared in better-off households.

Larger fish are chosen, preferably Trey ros, Trey chhdor, Trey chkok or Trey pruol (see pp 78, 79, 29, and 33). The chosen fish is washed, sometimes gutted, but not scaled. It is grilled over charcoal, being turned frequently but with care so that the whole of it is cooked through.

A second platter is prepared, of vegetables, green salad and aromatic leaves. The vegetables may be cucumber (peeled) and bean sprouts (well washed). Citronella and mint would be likely to figure among the aromatic leaves.

A sauce is prepared separately. The basis of it is the staple fish sauce, to which are added garlic, fresh chilli pepper, lime juice, galingale, roast peanuts, sugar, vinegar and coconut juice. Morsels of grilled fish and of the vegetables are wrapped in salad leaves and dipped in the sauce before being eaten.

MICCHA TRONG KROEUNG (decorated fish)

This, a recipe from the collection published by Princess Rasmi Sutharot, is a more elaborate confection.

A Trey ros (snakehead, page 78) is the chosen fish. Scale, wash, gut and behead it. Take out the bones and cut the body into pieces of 5 cm. Wash and dry the pieces, then fry them until they are of a good golden colour. Reserve them on a serving platter.

Meanwhile you have pounded in a mortar a mixture of the following ingredients: 3 dried chilli peppers; 1 soupspoonful of chopped citronella; 1 coffeespoonful of chopped fennel bulb; a pinch each of salt and pepper; 15 cloves of garlic; 12 shallots; 1 coffeespoonful of finely chopped galingale; 2 soupspoonfuls of grated coconut; 3 leaves of the kind of citrus tree called krauch soeuch (combawa to the French); and 3 sprigs of dill or parsley. The resulting powder is to be fried in 6 soupspoonfuls of pork fat "until it releases a delicious aroma", whereupon a little more salt, and sugar and fish sauce to taste are added. The pieces of fish are placed in this mixture and moved about until they are well coated; then served with a garnish of very finely chopped dill (or krauch soeuch leaves).

A-MOK

My friend Martine Dean asked her cook in Phnom Penh, Mr Chea Cheam, to make this Khmer speciality for me and to give me his recipe for it, which appears below. The quantities are for 12 people (but eating daintily and with other fare to follow).

2 kilos of any fish, in small pieces (Mr Cheam used snakehead)
3 stalks lemon grass, cut into tiny slices
100 grams shallots, cut up
50 grams dried chilli peppers, cut up
100 grams 'saffron' (the orange-coloured inside of the rhizome of a plant called romiet)
some kcheay, the rhizome of a trailing plant (**Alpinia sp**.) to which the Khmer are partial
combawa leaves (krauch soeuch) (leaves with a lemony taste and an unusual shape, as shown in the drawing below)
salt and pepper
leaves of cha phlou (these are larger leaves, dark green in colour, but any edible leaves of the right size will do)
coconut milk, extracted from the meat of 2 coconuts

Pound in a mortar the lemon grass, shallots, chilli peppers, 'saffron', kcheay, krauch soeuch leaves and salt and pepper. Mix the result with the pieces of fish and the coconut milk.

Make banana leaf cases (about 8 or 9 cm long, 5 cm wide and 3 cm deep, open on top) and place a cha phlou leaf in the bottom of each, where it will fit snugly Pour in the fish mixture so that each case is half full, with the pieces of fish sticking up slightly from their milky and aromatic sauce. Bake in the oven for 30 minutes.

RECIPES FROM VIETNAM

When Gavin Scott was Time correspondent in Saigon he was good enough to stage for us (the word stage is chosen deliberately, his rooftop patio having a theatrical effect) a fish dinner, by which I mean a dinner consisting solely of fish courses. Better still, we were able to watch his cook, Nguyễn Thị Tuyên from Cantho, prepare the dishes. Hence the next two recipes, each for 6 or 8 people.

CANH CHUA CÁ LÓC

Sour snakehead soup

2 fairly large snakehead, total weight 3 kilos
rendered pork fat or cooking oil
200 grams (peeled weight) tamarind
1 pineapple cut into small, thin pieces
1 fresh chilli pepper, finely sliced (or 2 if you like a hot dish)
leaves of ngò tây ⎫
leaves of Chinese parsley ⎬ cut very fine
green parts of spring onions ⎭

Cook the tamarind in plenty of water (about 2 litres) for 15 minutes. Meanwhile remove heads and tails from the fish, clean and skin them, and cut them into large sections (each fish divided into three).

Heat the pork fat or cooking oil in a large saucepan, add the pineapple and stir for a few minutes until the pineapple is half cooked. Add the pieces of fish and toss the contents of the pan around so that the pieces of fish and the bits of pineapple are mixed up. Wait until the fat or oil is really hot again, then strain the tamarind water into the saucepan. Leave the pan over a low flame for about 10 minutes, then bring it to the boil quickly, remove the scum which will form and take the pan off the fire.

The leaves and the green parts of the spring onions are to be added immediately before serving the soup, when the guests are already at the table. The soup is served with rice.

CÁ CHUI NƯỚNG   ('Flower trout' barbecued whole)

The Vietnamese use the charming name 'flower trout' for **Ophicephalus micropeltes** (page 79). Buy 3 fairly large ones, each about 40 - 45 cm long and weighing 1¼ kilos or nearly so. The other ingredients are :

partly rendered pork fat, or cooking oil
MSG
spring onions
peanuts
edible leaves, such as Bạc hà (a large-leafed mint), Tiá tô (a big leaf with a serrated edge), Rau húng (another minty one), Rau dăm (chinese parsley) and Rau diếp cá (literally leaf lettuce fish)
rice paper/coconut cream

(for the accompanying platters)
tomatoes
pineapple
small green bananas
carambola (khế, which looks a small ribbed cucumber and slices into a star shape)
cucumber
1½ kilos cooked pork (half fat, half lean)

(for the sauce)
3 tablespoonfuls vinegar
1 - 1½ teaspoonfuls fish sauce
½ fresh red pepper, sliced thinly
1 or 2 teaspoonfuls sugar
3 tablespoonfuls water

Have a charcoal fire hot and glowing.

Do not clean the fish, just wash them under the tap, then run bamboo splinters through their mouths and down the body to a distance of about 30 cm (to keep them straight) and place them on the grid over the glowing charcoal. For fish weighing about 1½ kilos each allow about 45 minutes.

Remove the fish from the fire. The skin will by now be thoroughly burned. Peel it off, exposing the flesh, and dress this with partly rendered pork fat (heat 200 grams of pork fat in the oven until it has mostly liquefied and keep this standing in a bowl for a few hours, with the surviving bits of fat still in it) or a suitable oil (olive oil does well) and MSG and finely chopped spring onion.

The next step is either to barbecue the fish, in this state, for another 20 minutes, or to finish them off in a pre-heated slow oven (say 275° F) for the same length of time. The peanuts are to be roasted or fried and sprinkled over the fish at the last minute when they are brought (still whole) to table. Nguyễn Thị Tuyên put them on a platter on their sides, each with a whole spring onion sticking vertically up from its mouth.

But this is not all. There must also be a circular platter with the edible leaves in the middle and a decorative arrangement surrounding them (thin wedge-shaped pieces of pineapple slice, thin half-rounds of tomato, thin slices of carambola and green banana and thin slices of cucumber). Then there should be another platter bearing the thinly sliced pork. In addition there must be the sauce (made by mixing the ingredients listed above) and a little pile for each guest of very thin rounds of rice paper, previously soaked in coconut cream. The rice paper is used to make a package of fish, pork, leaves and garnishing, which is wrapped up, dipped in the sauce and finally eaten.

CHẢ CÁ LÃO VỌNG

A speciality from Hanoi

Chả cá lão vọng means, literally, " grilled cut up fish meat of the old fisherman", and is the name of a fish restaurant in Hanoi. "Dans le temps", as they say, there were four such restaurants in the same street. They were popular eating places for young French officials, especially after the regular Saturday afternoon race meetings. Now only one survives, in the attic of a private house. It has a long history and was the best known of the four, having a reputation for entertaining artistic and intellectual customers, a task in which the lady who ran and still runs it was aided by numerous beautiful "daughters of the house".

The restaurant serves one fish dish, the «grilled cut up fish meat». The pieces of fish (usually catfish) are first grilled on bamboo skewers,then brought to the table in a pan of pork fat, sizzling over a charcoal brazier The guests help themselves, adding from side dishes mint leaves, (or Chinese parsley) and dill, spring onion, rice vermicelli, peanuts, slivers of chilli pepper and fish sauce.

I should add that, when supplies permit this, a rare and costly ingredient is used to give additional flavour to the dish. There is in S E Asia a water bug which I have been told is **Lethocerus indicus,** from live specimens of which a few drops of a glandular secretion may be obtained for use as a flavouring agent. It is the custom to serve it from a medicine dropper. This is an expensive ingredient anywhere, and certainly in Hanoi, whither live bugs have to be conveyed from the places where they can be found. The dish with this extravagant addition made to the fish sauce cost 15 dong a head when I had it in 1975.

APPENDIX
BIBLIOGRAPHY
INDEX

APPENDIX: THE PA BEUK

The genus **Pangasianodon** was established by Chevey in 1930 to accommodate the magnificent and mysterious Pa beuk, giant catfish of the Mekong. He distinguished it from the various species which belong to the genus **Pangasius** by the absence of teeth and certain other differences.

The validity of the genus has not been seriously questioned, but may be open to doubt for the following reason. It is known that certain large catfish have teeth when they are young and lose them as they grow old. Small specimens of the Pa beuk are never taken (or virtually never - there seem to have been one or two instances). Here, then, we have a toothless fish which appears to exist only in full-grown form, from about 1 metre 10 or so. It is tempting to explore the possibility that it is simply the adult version of a catfish which is known under another name when young and which has teeth in that state; and to suppose that one day the 'missing link', i.e. a specimen of intermediate size in the process of losing its teeth, will be taken. However, no one, to my knowledge, has made a plausible suggestion about which would be this other catfish which supposedly grows up to be the Pa beuk; and the notion flies in the face of popular belief about the Pa beuk, which insists strongly that it is a separate and wholly distinctive fish.

Myths about the Pa beuk

It is (or was) popularly believed that the male Pa beuk all lived permanently in Lake Tali in China, where they swam around resplendent in their golden scales, awaiting the females who laboured up the Mekong each year to join them for spawning. (It is hard to see how this myth could survive the regular catching in Laos of male Pa beuk, which could moreover be seen to have no scales, still less golden ones.)

Another myth connects the hollowing-out of the course of the Mekong, by a dragon-spirit, with the arrival of the first Pa beuk from the sea. To this day many Lao believe that the Pa beuk is essentially or was originally a marine fish, although there is no record of its ever having been seen in or near the sea.

The Pa beuk are believed by some to live in caves. There are in fact caves near the **Ang** referred to below, but there is no evidence that they connect with the Ang or are habitable by large fish. (A more plausible development of this myth consists in saying simply that the Pa beuk live in deep pools at the bottom of the river. Asking people how they account for the fact that small Pa beuk are never taken, I have on several occasions had the answer that the parent Pa beuk naturally keep the little ones close to them in these deep pools and that there could be no question of their being let out until they are grown up.)

The admirable article by Serène on Fishing and the Ang Festivities, cited in the bibliography, has more details of some of these myths, besides an eye-witness account of the principal rite connected with the Pa beuk, to which we now come.

Fishing rites

Until recently an elaborate ceremonial accompanied the annual fishing for the Pa beuk at a deep pool called Ang Tong Nong Chao (the Golden Basin or the Lord's Lake) in front of the village of Ban Ang, upstream from Vientiane. The fullest account of this ceremonial has been given by Giles, whose 21-page paper, cited in the bibliography, makes fascinating reading. "Each year at the season of the falling of the waters, the people living in the vicinity of the Golden Basin, the home of the Pla Buk [Giles uses the Thai name] join together for the purpose of catching these fish. The observances, rites and ceremonies in connection with this catching commence on the 8th waxing of the 3rd month and continue till the 12th waxing. The netting of these fish is caried out from dawn to midday every day, from the 12th to the 15th waxing of the moon. ... The ceremonies connected with the taking of these fish are ancient and have been performed from time immemorial, and carried out once a year. There are several important Spirit Chiefs who have the duty of guarding over that portion of the river ... who must be propitiated by offerings of food and drink in order to obtain their help and favour, before the catching of the fish can take place." After listing the spirit of Siri Mangala, the spirit known as the Golden Swan, the spirit Chao Dan and the spirit of the Golden Basin, Giles goes on to give all the details of the propitiatory rites. Thus the Spirit of the Golden Basin required a procession of boats conveying swords, water gourds, trays of betel-nuts and leaves, pieces of silver and of beeswax, green coconuts, sweetmeats, candles, incense tapers, sandalwood flowers, a gong and two flutes, all to be offered to the Spirit with suitable music and incantations.

A similar ceremonial attitude applied to the construction of boats and nets and to the manner of fishing. One wonders how the fishermen, preoccupied by the need to do everything right, could devote the necessary attention to the actual catching of a fish. They would be further distracted by the requirement that they should hurl abuse at each other throughout the fishing. "O, bald-headed fool, O, ancients in thy dotage. A dog shall lay with thy mother. I will lay with thy mother. O, Friend, let me lay with thy wife ... " And so on. Yet fish were caught. The popular story is that these ceremonies died out because the appearance of motor boats on the river disturbed the conditions which had previously encouraged the Pa beuk to make the Ang into a sort of headquarters.

Although the rites are no longer observed, popular belief in the magic nature of the fish persists. It is still sometimes called Pa phi, meaning spirit or devil fish. And people at Luang Prabang still relate a story about an occasion many years ago when the present King of Laos caught a Pa beuk and was advised to cut it up on the spot so that the local Phi (spirit) could eat some. His Majesty preferred to take it first to a nearby village; but the engine of his boat caught fire on the way. This, it is made clear, was only to be expected.

Recent Catches

Little is known about the numbers of Pa beuk caught in the distant past. If Pavie is to be believed, the annual catch in Cambodia amounted to thousands. But I have found no comparable figures for Laos. Very few records seem to have been kept, even for the recent past. The general impression which is obtained from talking to interested people in Laos is that the fishery has declined steadily in the last two decades.

Thus I have been told that at Luang Prabang, in the old days (i.e. ten years ago or more), about a dozen Pa beuk were taken each year, and several more at Hak Mak Nao nearby. But by 1968 the catch had dwindled to 3. In 1969 only 1 was taken. 2 were caught in 1970, 1 in 1971 and none at all in 1972, 1973 and 1974 (although in 1974 I heard of one being caught at a place near Mung Nane, 70 kilometres from Luang Prabang). The fishermen at Ban Xieng Mene (the village across the river from Luang Prabang, whence the Pa beuk fishery was carried out) are inclined to ascribe the change to modifications of the river bed, which have occurred naturally and have removed the favourable conditions which used to exist for the fishery.

From Paksane down to the Cambodian frontier there seem to have been virtually no catches of Pa beuk for a long time.

At Vientiane the position is obscure. The lady who normally sells Pa beuk, when they are taken, in the Morning Market at Vientiane has said that something like 30 still pass through her hands annually, some in the spring and quite a lot in the last few months of the year. But no record is kept. I have myself witnessed the arrival of a Pa beuk at the market at 0630 and have observed that by 0730 all of it was sold and no trace left save for a few bloodstains.

Fortunately, the information available from Ban Houei Sai is more precise, partly because the fishery there is strictly seasonal; it lasts for about six weeks in the period April/May, when the waters of the Mekong are just starting to rise again. The Pa beuk taken at Houei Sai are always going upstream, and the females are always with eggs. (This fits in with the popular idea that the Pa beuk go to spawn in a lake in China.) The river runs wide and shallow for a couple of kilometres below Houei Sai, and it is here that the fishery takes place. A pirogue manned by four fishermen puts out from one bank and crosses almost to the other, paying out as it goes a large-meshed net which is big enough to stretch across the river and to hang down almost to the river bed. A buoy is attached to the end paid out first, and there are floats on the net at intervals thereafter. When the net is arrayed across the river at right angles to it, it is allowed to drift downstream with the pirogue. The fishermen hope that a Pa beuk coming upstream will run into it. This does not happen very often. Having taken part in this fishery myself, I can vouch for the tedium of hauling in the heavy net, going back upstream, paying it out again, drifting down, then hauling it in and so on through a long day (or night). The average catch in recent years has been between 20 and 30. 1973 was a good year; 34 were taken. But 1974 was a poor year; there were fewer fishermen at work and only 14 Pa beuk were caught, as follows (records kindly compiled for me by Mr Bounchanh, under the direction of Mr Jack Huxtable, Area Coordinator for USAID):

Fisherman	Time / Date	Weight of fish	Sex
AY TA	0600 20 April	160 kilos	M
AY SOM	0700 22 April	170 kilos	M
AY TA	1300 25 April	155 kilos	M
AY SONG	1800 29 April	140 kilos	M
AY SONG	1500 30 April	145 kilos	M
*TASSENG THONGDY	1300 3 May	170 kilos	M
AY CHAN	1000 6 May	160 kilos	M
*TASSENG THONGDY	1400 7 May	180 kilos	M
AY SOM	1400 8 May	200 kilos	M
AY PENG	1400 9 May	145 kilos	M
THIT BOUNTHANH	0600 11 May	150 kilos	M
*LUNG BOUNTHANH	0800 14 May	165 kilos	F
AY SONG	0600 16 May	160 kilos	F
AY TA	1300 21 May	135 kilos	M

The fishermen marked with an asterisk are Lao, from Ban Houei Sai; the others are Thai from the opposite bank. The weights given are close estimates. Lengths were not recorded.

The traditional way of measuring the Pa beuk in Laos is by noting how much of the fish protrudes through the mesh of the special net in which it is taken. If the head and forepart of the body, up to the dorsal fin, go through, the fish caught is of the small size known as Pa hev. The next size up is a fish which has its whole head through the mesh, but no more. A larger size still has only the nose, from the eye forward, protruding. And the largest of all (known as Pa pok) doesn't even get its nose through the net!

This all sounds rather primitive and inexact, but it does not seem so bad a method after one has vainly searched in a Lao village or market for scales capable of weighing a whole fish.

More Questions, mostly about Migratory Journeys

I have mentioned above some of the puzzles about the Pa beuk. But there are many more, some of which I list below.

1) How long does a Pa beuk take to reach adult size? A Thai expert (Mr Tiraphan Pookaswan, see bibliography) has calculated that a fish of just over 2 metres in length would be in its sixth year. But I have heard other views which suggest that such a fish might be 12 years old or more.

2) How does spawning take place? (Mr Pookaswan quotes a fishermen as stating that a female fish, 2.30 metres long, contained ovaries weighing 16 kilos, comprising millions of eggs 5 mm in diameter; and himself records that a male of the same length had testes 43 cm long which weighed 140 grams.)

3) Why are small Pa beuk not taken? Could it be that they descend, when small, from the spawning grounds at the time when the Mekong is high, when it would be impossible to catch them, and that they then shelter in deep pools until they are fully grown?

4) Do the adults make long or short journeys to spawning grounds? Can it be that they all, from all parts of the Mekong, go all the way up to China to spawn? Or are there a number of colonies of Pa beuk in different parts of the Mekong, each of which has a spawning ground at no great distance? On the latter hypothesis the Pa beuk taken at Ban Houei Sai (and evidently on their way to spawn) could be making a relatively short journey. On the former they might have come from Cambodia.

5) But could a Pa beuk come from Cambodia to Laos? What about the Falls of Khong? Some say that the Pa beuk could never have traversed these. Others say that it was possible in the past but has not been so since the one feasible passage was altered by man to facilitate the

passage of boats. Yet others say that there has never been and is not now a problem, since there are subsidiary passages flanking the Falls which could be negotiated even by the largest fish.

6) Why is it that the Pa beuk taken in Cambodia and the south of Laos are reputedly not very good to eat, being rather fat, whereas those taken further upstream are delicious? Could this be because of the beneficial effects of a long spawning migration? Or should it be explained on the basis that the food in Cambodia, e.g. in the Tonle Sap, is more plentiful and rich?

BIBLIOGRAPHY

ARCHAIMBAULT, Charles: **Les techniques rituelles de la pêche du palo'm au Laos**: an essay of 1958 reprinted in the author's Structures religieuses Lao: Editions Vithagna, Vientiane, 1973

BARDACH, John E.: **Report on Fisheries in Cambodia**: USOM, Cambodia, undated but circa 1960

BOURRET, René: **Les Tortues de l'Indochine**: Note No. 38 de l'Institut Océanographique de l'Indochine: Station Maritime de Cauda, 1941

CHEVEY, P.: **Sur un nouveau silure géant du bassin du Mekong, Pangasianodon gigas nov. g. nov. sp** : Bulletin of the Zoological Society of France, vol. 55, pp 536-542: Paris, 1930

CHEVEY, P.: **Poissons des campagnes du 'de Lanessan' (1925-29)**: Travaux de l'Institut Océanographique de l'Indochine, 4ème Mémoire: Gouvernement Général de l'Indochine, 1932

CHEVEY, P. and LEMASSON, L.: **Contribution à l'étude des poissons des eaux douces Tonkinoises**: Note No. 33 of the Institut Océanographique de l'Indochine: Saigon, 1937

CHEVEY, P. and LE POULAIN, F. : **Rapport préliminaire sur la pêche dans les eaux douces cambodgiennes**: extrait du Bulletin Economique de l'Indochine, Année 1939, Fascicules 1 et 2

CHRUNG, Taing Meng: **Contribution à l'étude des Perciformes d'eau douce du Cambodge**: Mémoire de fin d'études, Université des Sciences Agronomiques, Phnom Penh, 1972

DAY, Francis: **The Fishes of India, Burma and Ceylon**: London, Quaritch (vol. 1 1876, vol. 2 1878, supplement 1888)

DAY, Francis: **The Fauna of British India, including Ceylon and Burma, Fishes**, Vols 1 and 2: London 1889

FILY, M. : **Report on Fisheries Technology in the Great Lake and the Tonle Sap, 1962-1963**: National Museum of Natural History, Paris

GILES, F.H.: **An Account of the Ceremonies and Rites performed when catching the Pla Buk** . . . : Journal of the Siam Society. volume 20, pp 91-113: 1935

HAMILTON, Francis: **An Account of the Fishes found in the River Ganges and its branches**: Edinburgh, 1822

HELLEI, Professor Andras: **Les coutûmes alimentaires Khmères**: No. 3 of the Etudes Statistiques of the Institut National de la Statistique et des Recherches Economiques: Phnom Penh, 1973

KANCHANANAGA, Suraphong: **Resources and Products of Thailand**: Siam Communications Ltd, Bangkok, 1973

KHIN, U: **Fisheries in Burma**: Government of the Union of Burma, Rangoon: 1948

KURONUMA, K.: **A Check-list of Fishes of Vietnam**: USOM, Vietnam: Saigon, 1961

LAO WOMEN'S ASSOCIATION: **Lao Cooking** (in Lao): Vientiane, undated

LLOZE, René: **Les poissons des eaux continentales du Cambodge et leur pêche**: Phnom Penh, 1964

MAXWELL, C.N.: **Malayan Fishes**: Methodist Publishing House, Singapore, 1921

MILLER, Jill Nhu Huong: **Vietnamese Cookery**: Charles E. Tuttle Company, Tokyo, 1968

MACKIE, I.M., HARDY, R. and HOBBS, G.: **Fermented Fish Products**: FAO Fisheries Reports, No. 100: FAO, Rome, 1971

NATIVIDAD, Bella Flor G.: **Lao Foods**: Vientiane, 1973 (this booklet contains a number of fish recipes translated from the Lao cookery book cited under Lao Women's Association above)

NGUYEN VIET TRUANG, NOBUYUKI KAWAMOTO and TRAN THI TUY-HOA: **Illustrations of Some Freshwater Fishes of the Mekong Delta, Vietnam**: University of Cantho: 1972

PANTULU, V.R.: **Fishery Problems and Opportunities in the Mekong**: (reprinted from Geophysical Monograph Series No. 17): American Geophysical Union, Washington DC, 1973

PAVIE, Auguste: Mission Pavie Indo-Chine 1879-1895: Etudes diverses, III, **Recherches sur l'histoire naturelle de l'Indochine orientale, vol. 3, Poissons**: Paris, 1904

PING, Phia: Two unpublished **Cahiers of Recipes**, numbered 2 and 3, containing manuscript recipes numbered from 1 to 114

POOKASWAN, Tiraphan: **Some Fish Species Found in the Mekong River**: Inland Fisheries Division, Department of Fisheries, Government of Thailand: Bangkok, 1968

POOKASWAN, Tiraphan: **Pangasianodon gigas Chevey**: Bulletin No. 7, April 1969, of the Inland Fishery Division of the Department of Fisheries, Bangkok, Thailand.

PUDSADORN, S.: **Hunt for Pangasianodon**: Thai Fish. Gaz. 20 (2), pp 225-231 (in Thai): 1967

SAURIN, Hem: **Contribution à l'étude systématique des poissons pêchés au 'day'**: Mémoire de fin d'études, Université des Sciences Agronomiques, Phnom Penh, 1971

SERENE, R.: **Fishing and the Ang Festivities**: in **Kingdom of Laos**, special issue of France-Asie, English version published 1959

SERENE, R.: **Sur la faune ichthyologique du Laos**: document IPFC/C51/TECH 49 of the 3rd Meeting of the Indo-Pacific Fisheries Council, at Madras: 1951

SERENE, R.: **Les engins de pêche des Laotiens**: in **Bulletin des Amis du Laos**, 3rd year, No. 3, 1939

SIDTHIMUNKA, Ariya: **A Report on the Fisheries Surveys of the Mekong River in the Vicinity of the Pa Mong Dam site**: Inland Fisheries Division, Department of Fisheries, Government of Thailand: Bangkok, 1970

SMITH, H.M.: **The Freshwater Fishes of Siam, or Thailand**, Bulletin No. 188 of the United States National Museum: Washington, 1945

SOBHANA, S. A. R. La Princesse Rasmi: **Le Guide Culinaire Cambodgien**: published for the American Women's Club of Cambodia by USIS, Phnom Penh, 1963

SONAKUL, Sibpan: **Everyday Siamese Dishes**: Sixth Edition, Bangkok, 1971

SUVATTI, Chote: **Fauna of Thailand**, second edition: Applied Scientific Research Corporation of Thailand, 1967

TAKI, Y.: **Notes on a collection of fishes from lowland Laos**: USAID Mision to Laos: Vientiane, 1968

TAKI, Y.: **Fishes of The Lao Mekong Basin**: USAID Mission to Laos: Vientiane, 1974

TENG, UNG: **Les aliments usuels au Cambodge**: thesis published by the Université Royale, Phnom Penh, 1967

TIRANT, G.: Notes sur les poissons de la Basse-Cochinchine et du Cambodge, in **Excursions et Reconnaissances**, Vols IX and X, Saigon, 1885

TRAN-NGOC-LOI and NGUYEN-CHAU: Les poissons d'importance commerciale au Vietnam in **Bulletin de la Société des Etudes Indochinoises**, N.S. Tome XXXIX, No. 3, 3ème trimestre, 1964

VIDAL, Jules: **Noms vernaculaires de plantes (Lao, Meo, Kha) en usage au Laos**: Ecole Française d'Extrême-Orient, Paris, 1959

VIPULYA, MOM CHAO: **Notes on Rod Fishing in Bangkok**: Journal of the Natural History Society of Siam, vol 6, pp 223-227: 1923

WOMEN'S SOCIETY OF CHRISTIAN SERVICE OF THE METHODIST ENGLISH CHURCH: **Rangoon International Cookbook**: Rangoon, 3rd edition, 1962

INDEX

The main index gives all the fish names which occur in the catalogue. It is followed by a supplementary index which gives recipe titles.

Acanthopsis choirorhynchos 47
Anabantidae 73
Anabas testudineus 74
Antong 89
Archerfish 98
Aristichthys nobilis 50
Aruan 78

Bagarius bagarius 72
Bagroides macracanthus 68
Barb 29, 30, 34, 35, 36, 37, 40
Barb, bony-lipped 38, 39
Barilius bola 32
Barilius guttatus 32
Batagur baska 96
Begahak 53
Belida 86
Belodontichthys dinema 53
Belontok 84
Belut 89
Betok 74
Betutu 84
Betta splendens 97
Big-head carp 50
Black carp 42
Black 'shark' 42
Boalla 43
Bony-lipped barb 38, 39
Botia hymenophysa 46
Butter catfish 54

Cá ba xa 62
Cá bông 79

Cá bống 84
Cá chạch lấu 88
Cá chài 24
Cá chấm trắng 49
Cá chành dục 80
Cá chến 72
Cá chép 48
Cá chốt 68
Cá chốt bông 69
Cá chốt là 71
Cá cốc 29
Cá còm 86
Cá đănh 37
Cá đở mang 36
Cá đuối 90
Cá duồng bay 30
Cá ét 42
Cá gáy 48
Cá he 28, 35
Cá heo 46, 47
Cá hố 27
Cá hường vện 81
Cá kết 57
Cá lăng 70
Cá lành canh 20
Cá leo 52
Cá linh bản 40
Cá linh tía 41
Callichrous bimaculatus 54
Cá lóc 78
Cá lòng tong 22
Cá lòng tong miếng 23
Cá mè 38, 39

Cá mòi dầu 92
Cá ngựa 26
Cá nhái 93
Cá phi 83
Cá rô đồng 74
Cá rói 33
Cá rô thia 82
Carp 19, 28, 31, 33, 41, 43, 44
Carp, big-head 50
Carp, black 42
Carp, common 48
Carp, giant Siamese 27
Carp, grass 49
Carp, silver 50
Cá rựa 21
Cá sát bo 61
Cá sát rắn 76
Cá sửu 94
Cá tai tượng 77
Catfish 51 to 72, passim
Cá thát lát 87
Catlocarpio siamensis 27
Cá tra 62
Cá tra chuột 60
Cá trà sọc 31
Cá trà vinh 34
Cá trèn bầu 54
Cá trèn mo 55
Cá trèn trắng 53, 58
Cá trê vàng 59
Cá vồ 64
Cá vồ cò 65
Cá xanh kỳ 63
Channa striata 78
Chela oxygastroides 20
Chinese carp 49
Chitala 86
Chow hu 49
Cichlidae 83
Cirrhinus auratus 33
Cirrhinus jullieni 33
Cirrhinus lineatus 33
Cirrhinus microlepis 33
Clarias batrachus 58
Clarias macrocephalus 59

Climbing perch 74
Clupea kanagurta 92
Clupea thibeaudeaui 92
Cobitidae 19
Common carp 48
Con luon 89
Cosmochilus harmandi 30
Croaker 94
Ctenopharyngodon idellus 49
Cyclocheilichthys apogon 29
Cyclocheilichthys enoplos 29
Cyclocheilichthys repasson 29
Cynoglossus 91
Cyprinidae 19
Cyprinus carpio 19, 48

Dangila siamensis 40
Dasyatis sp. 90
Datnioides microlepis 81
Djambal 63
Djuara 63
Drum 94
Dugong 99

Eel, spiny 88
Eel, swamp 89
Electric eels 100
Eleotridae 73
Esomus metallicus 22

Featherback 86, 87
Fighting fish 97
Fluta alba 89
Freshwater 'shark' 52
Freshwater shrimp 95
Freshwater turtle 96

Gar fish 93
Giant catfish 66
Giant Siamese carp 27
Glass fish 20
Goby 84
Goramy 77
Goramy-lay 76
Couramy 77

Grass carp 49
Gyrinocheilus aymonieri 45

Hampala dispar 26
Hampala macrolepidota 26
Heel-gorya 43
Helicophagus waandersi 60
Hemisilurus heterorhynchus 56
Herring 92
Heterobagrus bocourti 71
Hilsa kanagurta 92
Hypophthalmichthys molitrix 50

I'en 89
Ikan baung 70
Ikan laeh itam 54
Ikan lele 58

Jambal 52

Kampoes 95
Kanchrouk kraham 46
Kantheay 96
Koung 95
Kryptopterus apogon 57
Kryptopterus bicirrhis 55
Kryptopterus bleekeri 56
Kryptopterus cryptopterus 55

Labeo behri 44
Labeo chrysophekadion 42
Labeo dyocheilus 43
Labeo rohita 43
Labiobarbus lineatus 41
Lais 53
Lampam 35
Lalawak 34
Lawak 34
Lawang 63
Leiocassis siamemsis 60
Leptobarbus hoevenii 24
Loach 46, 47
Lobotidae 73
Lopis 86
Luciosoma bleekeri 23

Macrochirichthys macrochirus 21
Macrognathus aculeatus 88
Macrones nemurus 70
Macrones nigriceps 71
Mahseer 19, 28
Marotja 36
Mastacembelus armatus armatus 88
Mastacembelus armatus favus 88
Mata-merah 36
Mekongina erythrospila 44
Minnow 22, 23
Monopterus albus 89
Morulius chrysophekadion 42
Mystus cavasius 71
Mystus nemurus 70
Mystus nigriceps 71
Mystus rhegma 71
Mystus vittatus 71
Mystus wyckii 70

Nandidae 73
Nga-but 52
Nga-bye-ma 74
Nga-dok 28
Nga-khoo 58
Nga-lawa 32
Nga-maun-ma 72
Nga-myit-chin 43
Nga-nu-than 54
Nga-pe 87
Nga-pe-gone 86
Nga-phoung-yoe 93
Nga-thinbawmo 88
Nga-thine 27
Nga-yaing-kyetchay 71
Nga-yan 78
Nga-yan-gaungdo 80
Nga-zin 71
Notopterus blanci 87
Notopterus chitala 86
Notopterus notopterus 87

Ompok bimaculatus 54
Ophicephalidae 73
Ophicephalus gachua 80

Ophicephalus lucius 80
Ophicephalus micropeltes 79
Ophicephalus striatus 78
Osphronemus goramy 77
Osteochilus hasseltii 38
Osteochilus lini 38
Osteochilus melanopleura 39
Osteochilus prosemion 39
Osteochilus vittatus 38
Oxyeleotris marmoratus 84
Oxygaster oxygasteroides oxygasteroides 20

Pa beuk 66
Pa bou 84
Pa chow hu 49
Pa dan deng 56
Paddy eel 89
Pa do 79
Pa douk 58, 59
Pa eun 31
Pa eun mo 27
Pa fa lai 90
Pa gneun 50
Pa gnon 61
Pa gnon tiun 68
Pa hak kuey 45
Pa hang fa 21
Pa hien 28
Pa hoa gnay 50
Pa hou mat 64
Pa it 47
Pa ka 82
Pa ka dout 76
Pa ka gneng 68, 71
Pa ka gneng pho 71
Pa ka gneng po 68
Pa kang 80
Pa kat 97
Pa katheung 68
Pa katung 93
Pa keng 39
Pa kha 99
Pa khao 36, 52
Pa khao i thai 29
Pa khao mon 38

Pa khe 72
Pa khe khao 72
Pa khe leuam 72
Pa kheng 74
Pa kheo kai 46
Pa kheung 70
Pa khi hia 69
Pa kho 78
Pa khop 53
Pa khoui lam 41
Pa khoun 52
Pa kin gna 49
Pa ko 45
Pa kor 45
Pa kot 70
Pa kouang 94
Pa koum 40
Pa lai 89
Pa lat 88
Pa leum 65
Pa leuan fai 35
Pa lian hu 50
Pa ling 61, 62
Pa lot 88
Pa mak phang 92
Pa men 77
Pa meo 98
Pa mou 46
Pa mou mang 46
Pa nai 48
Pa nang 57
Pa nay 40
Pangasidae 60
Pangasionodon gigas 66
Pangasius larnaudii 64
Pangasius nasutus 62
Pangasius pangasius 63
Pangasius sanitwongsei 65
Pangasius siamensis 61
Pa nin 83
Pa nok khao 39
Pa nou 60
Pa pak 34
Pa pak kham 35

Pa pak kum 34
Pa pao 99
Pa pe 91
Pa pha ong 96
Pa phia 42
Pa pi kai 55
Pa pho 62
Pa phom 62
Pa phone 33
Pa phong 24
Pa phong khunk 25
Pa phong long 25
Pa pok 36
Pa sa gneng mo 68
Pa sa ho 27
Pa sa i 44
Pa sa kang 37
Pa sa lit 76
Pa sa nak 32
Pa sa ngoua 56
Pa sa thong 93
Pa seua 81
Pa seuam 54, 55, 56
Pa sieu 22
Pa sieu ao 23
Pa sieu dok khao 23
Pa sieu khao 23
Pa sieu yuok 23
Pasir 47
Pa song hu 50
Pa souei 63
Pa soi 20, 33
Pa sout 26
Pa tchiuk 29, 30
Pa tep 20
Pa thep 20
Pa tiok 29, 30
Pa tiok gniou 29
Pa tong 86, 87
Pa va 43
Pa va ho kham 44
Pa va khai 44
Pa va na no 44
Pa va sa i 44
Pa vien fai 35

Pepuyu 74
Perch-like fish 73
Percidae 73
Pla ai ao 23
Pla ai ba 24
Pla ao 23
Pla ba 24
Pla bai mai 76
Pla ben 90
Pla biew 53
Pla bu 84
Pla bua 43
Pla buk 66
Pla bu sai 84
Pla chado 79
Pla chalat 87
Pla cha on 54
Pla chon 78
Pla chorn 78
Pla dab lao 21
Pla deng 56, 57
Pla dog jok 30
Pla dogmag 32
Pla dong deng 56
Pla duk dan 58
Pla duk uey 59
Pla hang deng 24
Pla hang kai 55
Pla hang pan 86
Pla hao smoh muk 36
Pla itub 52
Pla ituk 52
Pla ka 42
Pla kaben 90
Pla kadi mor 76
Pla kae 72
Pla kahae tong 35
Pla kaho 27
Pla kamang 37
Pla kam cham 36
Pla kang 80
Pla kang buan 53
Pla kapien tong 35
Pla kasoob 26
Pla kasoop 26

Pla kasoop khao 26
Pla kathing 88
Pla katung heo 93
Pla kayeng 71
Pla kayeng bai khao 71
Pla kayeng hin 69
Pla kayeng tong 71
Pla kayeng wang 68
Pla khao 52
Pla khi khom 38
Pla kien 28
Pla klet tee 40
Pla kluey 47
Pla kot 70
Pla kot hin 69
Pla kot kae 72
Pla krai 86
Pla krayok 55
Pla lal 89
Pla lampam 35
Pla lao tong 41
Pla liam 37
Pla lin kwai 91
Pla lin ma 91
Pla lot 88
Pla ma 94
Pla melang pu 79
Pla min 77
Pla mong kroi 92
Pla mood 45
Pla mor 74
Pla mor chang yieb 82
Pla mu 46
Pla mu kang lai 46
Pla mu khao 46
Pla nam lang 29, 30
Pla nang ao 32
Pla nang klet 40
Pla neua on 54, 55
Pla nuan chan 33
Pla paep 20
Pla paep khao 20
Pla pak lal 45
Pla pak pra 21
Pla patong 82

Pla peek 34
Pla piing 45
Pla pok 36
Pla prom 30
Pla prom hua men 39
Pla raet 77
Pla rak kluey 45
Pla sa 41
Pla sadet 74
Pla sai 47
Pla sai tan 29
Pla saiyu 62
Pla salat 87
Pla salid 76
Pla sangawart 61
Pla sangawart leung 61
Pla sawai 63
Pla sawai nu 60
Pla seua taw 81
Pla siew 22
Pla soi nok khao 38
Pla son sai 47
Pla soob 26
Pla soop 26
Pla ta deng 41
Pla takok 29, 30
Pla tapak 34
Pla tapien khao 34
Pla tapien sai 29
Pla tepo 64
Pla thepa 65
Pla tu bo 38
Pla tuk 52
Pla wien 28
Pla yeesok 31
Pla yeng 71
Pristolepis fasciatus 82
Probarbus jullieni 31
Pseudosciaena soldado 94
Pteropangasius cultratus 61
Puffer fish 99
Puntioplites proctozysron 37
Puntius altus 35
Puntius daruphani 34
Puntius gonionotus 31

Puntius javanicus 34
Puntius orphoides 36
Puntius rubripinna 36
Puntius schwanenfeldii 35
Puntius waandersi 37

Rasbora myersi 22
River dragons 100

Sciaenidae 94
Sebarau 26
Sepat Siam 76
'Shark', black 42
Sheatfish 55, 56, 57
Shrimp, freshwater 95
Siamese carp, giant 27
Si hatam 42
Silver carp 50
Singgal 70
Snakehead 78, 79, 80
Snakeskin gouramy 76
Sole 91
Spiny eel 88
Sting-ray 90
Striped nanda 82
Synaptura harmandi 91
Swamp eel 89

Tapab nam 96
Tapah 52
Temelian 31
Thynnichthys thynnoides 40
Tilan 88
Tilapia 83
Tilapia mossambica 83
Tilapia nilotica 83
Toman 78, 70
Tor sp. 28
Tor tambroides 28
Tor tor 28
Toxotes jaculatrix 98
Toxotes microlepis 98
Trey ampil tum 36
Trey andat chhké 91
Trey andeng 58

Trey bândaul chek 45
Trey chakèng 37
Trey changvar 22
Trey chek tum 68
Trey chhdor 79
Trey chhlaing 70
Trey chhlang 70
Trey chhlaunh 88
Trey chkok 29
Trey chpin 34
Trey chviet siach 61
Trey damrey 84
Trey dang dau 23
Trey dang khténg 21
Trey diep 79
Trey ka-êk 42
Trey kahě 35
Trey kaho 27
Trey kạmpoul bay 30
Trey kamphlieng samré 76
Trey kânchos chhnaut 71
Trey kânchos thmâr 69
Trey kanchrut 46
Trey kantho 76
Trey kantrâp 82
Trey kaor 28
Trey ke 62
Trey kebak 92
Trey kès 57
Trey kham 26
Trey khchung 88
Trey kla 81
Trey klang hay 53
Trey khmau 26
Trey kolréang 27
Trey krabey 72
Trey krâmâm 54
Trey kranh 74
Trey kray 86
Trey kros 38
Trey kros memay 40
Trey kroum 39
Trey lenh 40
Trey linh 40
Trey pabel 90

Trey palung 92
Trey pama 94
Trey pau 64
Trey phtoung 93
Trey po 64
Trey po pruy 65
Trey pra 63
Trey pra-kandor 60
Trey pråloung 24
Trey proul 33
Trey pruol 33
Trey ras 78
Trey reach 66
Trey riel 33
Trey romeas 77
Trey ros 78
Trey ruschek 47
Trey sanday 52
Trey slat 87
Trey slek russey 20

Trey sraka kdam 29
Trey sråka kéo 32
Trey srokchen 48, 49
Trey tråsåk 31
Trichogaster pectoralis 76
Trichogaster trichopterus 76
Trionyx cartilagineus 96
Trionyx steindachneri 96
Tripletail 81
Turtle, freshwater 96

Walking fish 74
Wallago attu 52
Wallago dinema 53
Wallagonia attu 52
Wallagonia miostoma 52
Wadonon 36

Xenentodon canciloides 93

INDEX OF RECIPES AND INGREDIENTS

Alipinia galanga 108
Allium cepa 110
Allium sativum 110
A-mok 175
Anethum sativus 115
Aubergine 109

Bai mak nao 106
Bai phak boua 111
Basil 116
Bean sprouts 112
Brassica sp. 117

Cá chui nướng 177
Canh chua cá lóc 176
Capsicum annuum 112
Capsicum frutescens 113
Careya sphaerica 119
Chả cá lão vọng 178
Chilli peppers 113
Chinese parsley 114
Citronella 106
Citrus hystrix 106
Coconut cream 105
Coriander 114
Coriandrum sativum 114
Cymbopogon nardus 106

Dill 115

Eggplant 109
Eryngium foetidum 118

Fish sauce 104

Galingale 108
Garlic 110

Ginger 108
Gnu mak kheua 121
Green pepper 112

Hom 114
Hom boua heng 110
Ho mok pla lai 171
Houa phak boua 110, 111

Kaffir lime 106
Keng pa say 122
Keng phet pla douk 170
Keng som houa pa va sai het 123
Keng som pa 124
Keng tom yum pa kho 125
Kha 108
Kha ta deng 108
Khing 108
Khor trey 173
Khoua gnu pa leum 126
Knap pa 127, 128
Knap pa gnon 129
Koy pa 130
Koy tioum 130, 131

Lam i'en 132
Lap leo 136
Lap pa 134
Lap pa kheng 135
Lap tia 136
Lemon grass 106
Lettuce 117
Lon padek 138
Luk sin pa 139

Mak kham 106
Mak kheua 109

Mak kheua hamaa 109
Mak kheua poy 109
Mak kheng 109
Mak kheng khom 109
Mak khi hout 106
Mak phet heng 113
Mak phet kinou 113
Mak phet kuntsi 113
Mak phet nyai 113
Mak thua ngork 112
Mak thua nyao 109
Mam pa kor 140
Marsilea quadrifolia 119
Melothria heterophylla 118
Mentha sp. 116
Miccha trong kroeung 174
Mieng pa 140
Mint 116
Mohinga 169
Mok khay pa 141
Mok pa 142
Mok padek po kha 143
Mok pa fok 145
Mok pa fa lai 144
Monosodium glutamate (MSG) 104
Mung beans 112

Nam pa 104
Nung pa 146

Ocimum basilicum 116
Ocimum gratissimum 116
Ocimum menthaefolium 116
Ocimum sanctum 116
Onion 110
Or pa 147
Or pa sa ngoua 148

Pa chao 149
Padck 104
Padek pa beuk 67
Pa keng, Lahu recipe for 39
Pa pan 151
Papeda 106
Pa phao 152

Parsley 114
Parsley, Chinese 114
Pa sa ngoua tchun na som 153
Pa ten 154
Pepper, black 113
Peppers, chilli 113
Peppers, green 112
Pepper, white 113
Petroselinum crispum 114
Phak boua 110
Phak boua houa pom 110
Phak boua lai leung 111
Phak boua la pha 116
Phak boua leui 111
Phak boua nyai 110
Phak hom 114
Phak hom po 116
Phak hom pom 114
Phak hom thet 118
Phak I lout 117
Phak kadone 119
Phak kat khao 117
Phak kat kieo 117
Phak itu lao 116
Phak itu thai 116
Phak kankam 116
Phak pheo 119
Phak salat 117
Phak seum 116
Phak si 115
Phak tam nin 118
Phak thiem 110
Phak wen 119
Phan kieo padek 155
Phan pa kho 152
Phik 112
Phik noi 113
Phik thai 113
Ping pa 156
Piper nigrum 113
Piper sp. 117
Plahengpad 172
Pla priowan 172
Polygonum odoratum 110
Ponnc pa 157

Rice cakes 105

Samla mchou banle 173
Sa ton pa va 158
Scallion 111
Shallot 110
Sngor 25
Som khay pa beuk 67
Som khay pa eun 159
Som pa 160
Som pa beuk 67
Sousi pa 162
Sousi pa gnon 162
Spring onion 111
Sweet basil 116

Tamarind 106
Tamarindus indica 106
Tchun pa 163
Tieo pa ka tao 164
Tom khem pa 165
Tom tchéo 166
Trey aing 174

Vigna unguiculata 109

Yard-long bean 109

Zingiber officinale 108

ADDITIONS AND POSTSCRIPT

Since I have forgone the benefits of having an editor for this book, I may as well enjoy the consequent lack of discipline and append here some interesting matter which was excluded by reasons of time or space from the main body of the book; together with an exhortation, and a blank page on which the reader, responding thereto, may note my mistakes and omissions.

FISHING FOR THE PA KHO (a note with reference to page 78)

Although this book only deals occasionally and incidentally with fishing methods, I must mention one extraordinary way of fishing for the Pa kho which was related to me by Dr Phulsena. He recalls that, when he was a boy in the South, there was a certain field which during the rainy season became a 'floating field', since so much water came in underneath it that the whole of the topsoil and the vegetation thereon rested on a shallow subterranean lake. In these waters the Pa kho went about their business; and boys fished for them in the following manner. They cut a hole in the centre of the field, rather as Eskimos cut a fishing hole in the ice, to reach down to the water. Then, retiring each to a corner of the field, they would start to run in a clumping way towards the centre, causing the floating earth to shake. The Pa kho, alarmed, would swim before the noise towards the centre; but as they neared this they would be further alarmed by similar noises and vibrations closing in on them from other directions. Some at least, in their agitation, would seek an apparent means of escape by leaping up through the hole, to lie gasping on the ground, whence the boys could pick them up.

CAVE-DWELLING FISH NEAR THAKHEK

Phagna Nouphat Chounramany, Deputy for Thakhek, tells me that in the limestone caves near Thakhek are waters which harbour an unusual fish known as the Pa nyung (?) described as a cross between a catfish and an eel. These fish are sometimes caught in May/June, but never in large quantities. They measure up to 40 cm in length and the flesh is very fine. This may turn out to be a fish which is familiar in other places, but for the present I cannot associate the report with any species of which I have heard.

THE 'VELVET FISH'

This is the Pa bou (page 84). It is called the 'velvet fish' because it feels like velvet if handled under water. This velvet feel and the inoffensive character of the fish caused women in the South of Laos, in the olden days, to think that the Pa bou was under the protection of the Buddha; and for this reason, so Dr Pholsena tells me, they were unwilling to eat it. However, although the Pa bou is still often selected as the fish to be released in pagoda pools or into the Mekong on the occasion of a religious festival, the old inhibitions about eating it have tended to disappear. The Chinese have always loved it in rice soup and the fact that it is not bony helps.

TWO MORE FISH FOR INVESTIGATION

In the South, between Attabeu and Savannakhet, huge shoals of tiny little fish, only 1 cm long and very thin, are met at certain seasons. They are transparent and are called Pa keo (keo meaning glass). The people there regard them as a delicacy, especially in the form of Som pa keo.

Another fish about which I have been able to find out very little is the Pa fang, which is to be fished in shallow streams with sandy bottoms. The Pa fang are also tiny and are used for Mok pa fang and Som pa fang.

CHOOSING YOUR SNAKEHEAD

It will be apparent from pages 78 to 80 and from many of the recipes that the snakehead is among the very best of the fish of Laos, and that the Pa kho is perhaps the best of all. Dr Pholsena points out that it is worth knowing the difference between male and female. The male has a darker body and a longer head; the female a lighter body and a more rounded head. The female is the better to eat. Its flesh is richer and has a special taste and aroma which that of the male lacks. Dr Pholsena recalls that when he was a boy he used to see an elderly gentleman going round the market with a cane, which he used to indicate the choicest females, which were to be conveyed to his home forthwith. His example is one to follow.

PARTING WORDS

Sometimes, when an author solicits corrections, the reader has the feeling that these would not, despite the fair words of invitation, be welcome. Not so with me and with this book. I know very well that there are omissions and mistakes in it, and have a strong desire to put such things right in any future edition. I shall be most grateful for any help to this end, and may always be reached at the British Embassy, P O Box 224, Vientiane.

ADDITIONS TO THE SECOND IMPRESSION

I am glad to have received from various kind readers some corrections and some additional information. Both have been applied to the text where possible. But not all the new information could be fitted in; hence these further notes.

TRANSCRIPTION OF THAI AND LAO NAMES

Mr Justin Staples, formerly of Vientiane and now of Bangkok, has been good enough to remove some of the inconsistencies in my transcriptions of Lao and Thai names. Some remain, but may be justified on the basis that one should not depart too far from the methods of transcription traditionally used by writers on the fish of the region.
In this connection Mr Staples has pointed out that the French tradition, which has usually been followed in Laos, differs noticeably from the methods which have been used in Thailand, and that this can suggest to the English-speaking reader that Thai and Lao names for fish differ more than they really do. Thus the Giant catfish of the Mekong (page 66) is shown as Pa beuk in Lao and Pla buk in Thai. But in the Lao and Thai languages the words beuk and buk (sometimes also written bük) are identical.

GLASS FISH

Referring to the second paragraph on page 202, Mr Thiraphan Bhukaswan (the same as the Tiraphan Pookaswan cited in the Bibliography) has told me that the Pa keo is probably a fish of the genus **Corica**. «In Thai, we call the fish of this genus Pla keo (meaning glass) or Pla kra-jok (meaning glass or mirror). We found **Corica goniognathus** Bleeker abundant in the water bodies along the Mekong Basin, particularly in newly created reservoirs such as the Sirinthorn Reservoir in Ubon Ratchathani Province. This species gathers in huge shoals. The Thai fishermen catch them by using light attraction at night and collect them by using scoopnets. It is good for fermented fish (Pla ra, Pla dek, etc) and fish sauce.»

TURTLE (PA FA) LAP

Mr Philip Unger, working on the Nam Ngum Limnological Survey, had ample opportunities to study lakeside Lao cookery and sent me this recipe for making Lap pa from the meat of the freshwater turtle. He observed that the same recipe can be applied to the water monitor, **Varanus salvator**, which is useful to know.

Remove the carapace from the turtle and mince the turtle meat. Fry it quickly in a hot pan, using no oil. Let it cool, then pour lime juice over it and sprinkle on top some fish sauce, finely chopped onion, salt and pepper. The meat is then to be mixed with Khao khoua (uncooked rice which has been fried until golden and then pounded) and eaten with steamed rice.

HOW I COOK PA BEUK

I have enjoyed Pa beuk cooked in various Lao ways and by the other methods indicated on page 67. However, our favourite recipe has turned out to be none of these, but an adapted version of an Italian recipe for cooking tunny. I have been asked for this by several people, and set it down here in its adapted form.

Ragu di Pa beuk

1½ kilo Pa beuk, in one piece
fresh mint
4 cloves garlic
salt and pepper
flour

¾ kilo tomatoes, peeled and chopped
2½ wineglassfuls olive oil
1¼ wineglassfuls white wine
2 onions, sliced

Chop up finely 2 of the cloves of garlic. Make cuts in the piece of Pa beuk. Into each cut introduce a mint leaf and a little chopped garlic, salt and pepper. Sprinkle the whole piece of fish with more salt and pepper and with flour.

Heat the oil in a pan and brown the piece of fish. Pour the wine over the fish and carry on cooking until the wine is all gone. Then take out the fish and keep it hot in a second, deep pan.

Crush the remaining 2 cloves of garlic. Add them and the sliced onions to the juice remaining in the first pan. Brown them. Then pour the contents of the pan over the fish and cook it for another 5 minutes, turning it once. Next, add the tomatoes and 2½ wineglassfuls of hot water. Cook gently for a further 30 minutes.

The fish being cooked, take it out and cut it into thick slices. Pour some

of the sauce over these. Serve the rest of the sauce separately with the
rice which should accompany the fish to table.

EDIBLE BIVALVES

I had overlooked the existence of these in Laos until Mrs Suganuma, wife
of the Japanese Ambassador in Vientiane, sent me a tureen of clam broth,
explaining that it was made
from tiny clams, shown on
the right, which are found in
Laos. The shells are dark
brown, and go under the
name Ki in the Vientiane
market. Mrs Suganuma had
recognised them as the same
freshwater clams which are
an expensive delicacy in
Japan, and enjoys having
them for breakfast everyday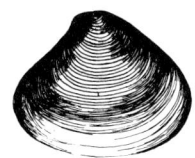
at trifling expense, for they are cheap in Laos. She assures me that they
are very good for the liver.

Mrs Suganuma's recipe for clam broth is as follows. Wash the clams very
well, then put them in water in a covered pot in a cool place. After an
hour, boil salted water in another pot, then wash the clams again and
add them to the boiling water. They will open quite soon. The broth may
then be eaten, and the clams too if you wish and have sufficient patience
to extract the tiny creatures from their shells. The amount of water may
be more or less, according to whether you like a weak or strong broth.
The broth sent to me was extremely strong; it had been made with enough
water to cover the clams and only a little to spare. I found it delicious so,
but most people would probably prefer a weaker version.

In the course of trying to establish the identity of this little clam (which
I have still not succeeded in doing) I learned that there are also much
larger bivalves in Laos, known as Kouang. These clams may measure as
much as 15 cm across and are found at various places in the Mekong.
They live in the sand and seem to prefer places where there are rocks
nearby. The one shown in the first drawing below is a specimen from the
Nam Ngum at Thangone. It lacks the sharp «crest» which projects up-
wards from the hinge of the shells and which can inflict a nasty cut on
incautious feet. The specimen in the second drawing came from the

Vientiane market.

The kouang are usually collected for the main purpose of making quicklime from their shells. However, the animals within are edible and are eaten. They may be baked in their shells in hot ashes (although when the shells open some of the hot ashes are likely to get in, which is a nuisance); or used for soup or just boiled. They are said to be somewhat tough, although I was assured at Thangone that the smaller specimens are sufficiently tender to make very good eating.

The interior of the shell of the kouang has a rosy tinge, which has prompted Mr One Sy to speculate about the possibility that these bivalves could be used for pearl culture. Rosy pearls are the most valuable. This is an interesting idea, especially since what I have heard about the kouang at Thangone suggests that they could be «planted» in beds of sand in shallow ponds. But, so far as I know, no - one has yet conducted any experiments.